more...
Michigan
Cooking
...and other things

by: Carole Eberly

Cover by William Kelley

Illustrations by Gerald Wykes

A NOTE

I feel like I'm coming home again writing this book. Four years ago I compiled my first book, MICHIGAN COOKING...AND OTHER THINGS never suspecting where the adventure would lead.

MORE MICHIGAN COOKING...AND OTHER THINGS is now the 9th book I've published since those days of peddling books door to door, selling to anyone who hesitated more than 15 seconds. Putting together MORE was as much fun as its parent book. So many people, including Bob Clock from Charlevoix, Jingo Viitala Vachon from Toivola in the U.P., Ginny Ebers from the Michigan Apple Committee, Judy Eldridge from Lansing and M. Dale Ogden of Walnut Creek, CA have helped with this book. And there are hundreds more who have helped without knowing it. My thanks to them--and to all of you.

But without the support of my terrific family, I wouldn't be sitting here writing this. I truly thank these two special people for making this book (as well as the others) possible.

Read on and enjoy--MORE MICHIGAN COOKING... AND OTHER THINGS.

Carole Eberly

ISBN 0-932296-07-6
First Edition May, 1981

CONTENTS

Tahquamenon Falls

Curwood Castle, Owosso

appetizers

snacks

beverages

CHEESE STRAWS

1 lb. Cheddar cheese	1 t salt
1 3/4 c. flour	1/4 lb. butter

Grate cheese and combine with other ingredients, beating until creamy. Divide dough in half. Roll to 1/4" thickness. Cut into 6" strips. Twist. Chill on ungreased cookie sheet in freezer 15 minutes. Bake at 350 degrees for 10-12 minutes. Makes 5-6 dozen.

*

CHEDDAR SPREAD

1 small onion, peeled and cut in wedges	1 3 oz.-pkg. cream cheese, softened
1 garlic clove, peeled	3/4 lb. cheddar cheese, cut in ½"
2 T mustard	cubes
2 T catsup	1/2 c. flat beer
4 drops Tabasco	

Put all ingredients in blender and mix well. Serve with crackers at your next party.

*

STUFFED CELERY

4 hard-boiled eggs, quartered	4 t lemon juice
2 4½-oz. cans deviled ham	2 t Worcestershire sauce
4 t honey	1/8 t Tabasco
	Large bunch celery

Blend all ingredients, except celery, in blender. Cut celery into 2" lengths. Fill with ham mixture. Chill.

*

PICKLED EGGS

12 hard-boiled eggs	1 t salt
1 1/2 c. white vinegar	6 whole cloves
1/2 c. water	1 bay leaf
1 c. sugar	1 onion, sliced

Peel eggs and place in narrow, deep jar. Bring vinegar, water, sugar, salt, cloves, and bay leaf to a boil. Reduce heat and simmer 5 minutes. Pour over eggs, making sure eggs are completely covered with the liquid. Place onion slices on top of eggs. Cover tightly, place in refrigerator and let stand several days. Eggs may be served whole, halved or sliced, plain or in sandwiches or salads.

*

BEEF JERKY

1-1 1/2 lb. flank steak	1/2 t garlic salt
1 1/2 t salt	1/4 t black pepper

Freeze steak partially for easy slicing. Trim off fat. Using a sharp knife, cut flank steak (with grain) into strips approximately 1/8 inch wide the length of steak. Combine salt, garlic salt and ground pepper. Sprinkle mixture over sliced meat. Arrange strips of meat, flat and close together on a wire rack in a shallow baking pan. Bake in a very slow oven (175 degrees) for 8-10 hours until dry and almost crisp. Cool on absorbent paper. Store in a covered container.

*

HAM IN EGGS

6 hard-boiled eggs
1/2 c. chopped, boiled ham
6 T crumbled blue
  cheese
1 T fresh minced onion

1/2 t lemon juice
1/4 c. mayonnaise
Salt and paprika to
  taste

Cut eggs in half lengthwise, and remove yolks. Mash yolks, add ham, cheese, onion, and mayonnaise. Season with salt and paprika. Pile filling back into egg whites.

*

VEGETABLE COTTAGE CHEESE SPREAD

Makes a great sandwich.

1 c. cottage cheese
1/4 c. grated carrot
1 T mayonnaise

1 t finely chopped
  green pepper
1/2 t chopped pimento
1/4 t onion salt

Mix ingredients together.

*

POTATO CHIPS

4 large potatoes, peeled
Oil

Salt

Slice potatoes with vegetable peeler. Blot well with paper towels. Heat oil in skillet. Add potatoes, a handful at a time. Fry until light golden brown, about 30 seconds. Drain on paper towels. Sprinkle with salt.

*

CHICKEN NUGGETS

4 whole chicken breasts,　1/2 t salt
　boned and skinned　　　1 t thyme
1/2 c. fine dry bread　　1 t basil
　crumbs　　　　　　　　1/2 c. melted butter
1/4 c. grated Parmesan
　cheese

Cut each breast half into nuggets, about
1¼" to 1½" square. Combine bread crumbs, cheese,
salt, thyme and basil. Dip chicken pieces in
melted butter and then in crumb mixture
Place in a single layer on foil-lined baking
sheet. Bake at 400 degrees until golden, about
10 minutes. Serve with picks. Makes 55 to 60
nuggets.

*

SPEEDY CARMEL CORN

2 1/2 qts. popcorn　　　1/4 c. water
2 T butter　　　　　　　2 T corn syrup (pre-
1 1/2 c. brown sugar　　　ferably dark)
　　　　　　　　　　　　1 t salt

Melt butter, sugar, water, corn syrup, and
salt. Stir till sugar dissolves, then cook
without stirring to soft ball stage (240 degrees).
Pour over 2 1/2 quarts popped corn and toss until
all corn is coated.

*

GARLIC POPCORN

6 c. popped corn　　　1 clove crushed garlic
1/4 c. butter, melted

Mix butter and garlic well. Pour over popcorn and mix.

*

CHOCOLATE POPCORN BALLS

1 1/4 c. sugar
1/2 c. cocoa
3/4 c. light corn syrup
2 t cider vinegar

1/8 t salt
2 T butter
1/4 c. evaporated
    milk
2 qts. popped corn

Combine sugar, cocoa, corn syrup, vinegar and salt in saucepan. Add butter and cook, stirring constantly, over low heat until sugar dissolves and mixture comes to a boil. Gradually add evaporated milk. Cook and stir over low heat until mixture reaches 265 degrees F. (hard-ball stage). Stir into popped corn. Butter hands, quickly roll large spoonfuls of mixture into 4-inch balls. Makes 20 balls.

*

CINNAMON POPCORN

6 c. popped corn
1 c. sugar
1/2 c. water
1/4 c. corn syrup

1 t vinegar
2 t ground cinnamon
1/4 t red food
    coloring
1 T butter

Heat sugar, water, corn syrup, and vinegar to boiling, stirring until sugar is dissolves. Cook to 300 degrees without stirring. Remove from heat and stir in cinnamon and food coloring. Pour over popcorn. Dot with butter. Mix well.

*

MINT TEA BATH

When your sunburned skin cries out for help after 6 hours on the beach, try this soothing bath. It looks terrible, but feels so good ---and it's completely edible (or is it drinkable?).

4 T loose tea	2 C. fresh mint leaves
5 c. boiling water	A warm tub of water

Steep tea in 4 cups boiling water for 10 minutes. Mix mint leaves and 1 c. boiling water in blender. Pour tea (with leaves) and mint in tub. Dive in.

*

HOT CHOCOLATE WITH MINT

1 T cocoa	1 c. hot milk
2 T sugar	1/8 t mint extract

Mix cocoa and sugar in a cup. Stir in hot milk and mint. Serves 1.

*

RASPBERRY MILK

1 pt. raspberries	1/2 t vanilla
3 T powdered sugar	1 1/2 c. milk

Mix all ingredients in blender. *Cheers!*

*

BLUEBERRY FROST

3/4 c. blueberries   1 c. cold milk
1/2 pt. raspberry ripple
   ice cream

   Combine blueberries, ice cream and milk in blender. Serves 2.

*

FROSTY APPLE SHAKE

1 qt. apple juice   1/2 t cinnamon
   (chilled)
1 pt. vanila ice cream
   (softened)

   Combine all ingredients in blender.

*

KIDS' ICE CREAM SODA

4 kids   1 qt. ice cream
4 straws   1 pt. soda pop
4 spoons   1 large bowl

   Find 4 kids. Give them each a straw and spoon. Put ice cream in bottom of large bowl. Slowly pour in pop. Stand back. *(Guaranteed to spread germs, but probably not much more than gathered by eating sand, sucking thumbs after petting the dog or gobbling the cookie that just fell on the floor.)*

*

PEACH CORDIAL

3 lbs. peaches,
  pitted & quartered
2 1/2 c. sugar
4 strips of lemon
  peel, 2" long

4 inches stick cinnamon
6 whole cloves
1 qt. whiskey

In gallon jar, combine peaches, sugar, lemon peel, and spices. Pour in whiskey, cover. Invert jar daily till sugar is dissolved, about 4 days. Place in cool, dark place for at least 2 months. Strain through cheesecloth before serving. Makes 1 1/2 quarts.

*

HOT MULLED PORT

3 c. cider
1/3 c. corn syrup
3 cinnamon sticks
2 t. whole cloves

1 orange
1 qt. cream port
1/2 c. brandy

Heat cider, corn syrup, and cinnamon sticks to boiling. Simmer 5 minutes. Stud orange with cloves. Add orange, port, and brandy to cider mixture. Simmer 5 minutes. Makes 2 quarts.

*

CHURCH MEETINGS

by Jingo Viitala Vachon

It used to be a real big event when a visiting missionary from the old country came to preach at the country church. Everybody and his uncle went.

Most of the people came by horse and wagon, but a few of the more progressive settlers had Model T's. I also recall a Reo touring car, and Iikka Tuttila had a conveyance that was a cross between a station wagon and a truck, and it was high enough for a man to walk into the open back end. There was a bench full length along each side for their eight kids to sit on.

Well, this particular evening (the services were always held in the evening, but I can't remember why) there was a regular exodus of farm families heading for the old log church, like pilgrims heading for Mecca.

As they neared the church, the latecomers saw the small cleared churchyard was full to overflowing, and they began parking along the side of the narrow country road.

Most of the farmers simply left their horses unhitched, trusting them to stand quietly and wait until the services were over, and they usually did, because the flies were always gone by evening.

Old Matti, however, had a high stepping young mare, and since he lived about six miles away, he didn't relish being left afoot, so he

---

CHURCH MEETINGS is a chapter from Jingo's book, SAGAS FROM SISULA, published by and available from the L'Anse Sentinel, L'Anse, MI 49946. The book is full of amusing stories by this Upper Peninsula Finnish Story-teller extraordinaire. Jingo, by the way, swears the tales are true.

tied the reins onto a steel rib in the back of
Iikka's truck.

After the services were over, coffee and baked
goodies were served in the basement and gossip was
exchanged by the women while farm topics were
shared by the men.

Iikka finally decided it was time to get his
family home, as the baby was beginning to fret,
and finding it impossible to round up all his kids
playing outside in the darkness, a neighbor of-
fered to ride them home later in his wagon and
drop them off in passing.

Iikka walked to the truck where his wife was
already nursing the baby and started the motor,
unaware of Matti's mare being hitched to the back.
Luckily he drove slow and easy on the way home,
and it wasn't until he walked around the back of
the truck that he heard the heavy labored breathing
of the mare.

It was funny in a sense, but Iikka sensed the
gravity too, and immediately unhitched and led the
exhausted mare into the barn where he wiped her
down and threw a blanket over her. Then and only
then did he drive back to the church where he met
old Matti trudging along the road, thinking his
mare had simply left for home.

A child was sometimes left behind uninten-
tionally, and not missed until home was reached.
The families were so large you couldn't keep track
of all the kids in the dark. It really made no
difference, and there was never any cause to worry.
You knew the child had ridden with someone else
and would stay overnight. With big families, it
was never unusual to see a strange young one in
bed with your own.

Funny things used to happen at these solemn
services, like the time a bat kept flying back and
forth over the congregation and threw everybody
into a turmoil until he flew out. Shades of Bela
Lugosi!

And the time a neighboring cat strolled in, right up to the preacher, leaped up on the altar rail and nonchalantly padded from one end to the other, then gracefully dropped down and strolled out, flicking his tail from side to side. The preacher never batted an eye, and kept right on with his sermon.

Once he almost did get flustered when Kalakoski's tame crow lit on the open window sill and cussed repeatedly during the sermon.

And the time a car horn got stuck at the peak of the sermon, and no one knew whose car it was, and almost half of the men ran out to shut it off! I guess the worst thing was when two dogs sneaked in and started a fight right in the middle of church, and a couple of guys had all they could do to separate them.

But I still think the funniest thing that happened was when Rapajarvi's hound started howling outside the door during the hymn singing. Even the stern faced preacher had an elusive twinkle in his eye. Maybe he rightly figured the hound had a better voice than some of the humans! Church meetings sure aren't the same anymore!

*   *   *

pickles
jams
sauces

KITCHEN FLOOR PICKLES

Pack glass gallon jar with small cucumbers. Add 2 T alum, 2 T salt, 1 c. whole mixed pickling spice and 4 c. vinegar. Fill up with water. Cap and let set for one month.

Remove pickles and rinse. Clean jar. Cut up pickles and put back in jar with 4 c. sugar. Cap and shake until cucumbers are covered with juice. Refrigerate. Eat up.

*

HOT GARLIC DILLS

Bunch of small-medium
   cucumbers
Dill
Garlic, mashed
Hot peppers
Alum

1 c. pickling salt
1 qt. vinegar
4 qts. water

In each canning jar put 2 heads dill, 1 garlic clove, 1 hot pepper, and 1 t alum. Pack tightly with cucumbers. Mix salt, vinegar, and water. Pour over cucumbers and seal. Process 5 minutes. Makes 4-5 quarts.

*

BEET RELISH

1 qt. chopped cooked
   beets
1 qt. chopped cabbage
1 c. chopped onions
1 c. chopped sweet red
   peppers

2 t. salt
1 T horseradish
1 1/2 c. sugar
3 c. vinegar

Mix all ingredients and simmer 10 minutes. Heat to boiling. Pack boiling hot mixture into sterilized jars. Process 15 minutes. Makes about 3 half-pints.

*

GREEN PEPPER RELISH

8 green peppers, finely ground
2 large hot chili peppers, finely ground
4 medium onions, finely ground
1/2 c. sugar
2/3 c. vinegar
1/3 c. water
1 t salt
1 t dillseed

In saucepan combine pepper and onion pulp; add boiling water to cover and let stand 5 minutes. Drain. Add remaining ingredients. Boil gently 5 minutes. Spoon relish mixture into hot, clean pint jars, leaving ½" head-space. Process 10 minutes. Makes 3 pints.

*

PEPPER-FRUIT RELISH

5 lbs. tomatoes, peeled, cored, and chopped (8 cups)
3 medium apples, peeled, cored, and chopped (3 cups)
3 medium pears, peeled, cored, and chopped (2 cups)
3 medium peaches, peeled, pitted, and chopped (1 1/2 cups)
1 1/2 c. chopped onion
1 medium green pepper, chopped
1 medium sweet red pepper, chopped
2 c. vinegar
2 c. sugar
1 T salt
1/4 c. mixed pickling spice

In large pot mix fruits and vegetables with vinegar, sugar, and salt. Tie pickling spice in a cheesecloth bag, add to mixture. Bring to boiling, boil, uncovered, 45 to 60 minutes or till reduced by half. Remove spice bag, pour mixture into hot, clean pint jars, leaving ½" head-space. Process 10 minutes. Makes 5 pints.

*

APPLE-BLUEBERRY CONSERVE

1 qt. chopped, tart apples	6 c. sugar
1 qt. blueberries	1/2 c. raisins
1/2 t cinnamon	1/4 c. lemon juice

Mix all ingredients, slowly heat to boiling, stirring occasionally, until sugar dissolves. Cook rapidly until thick, about 20 minutes, stirring frequently. Pour boiling mixture into sterilized jars. Process 10 minutes. Makes about 6 half-pints.

*

CANTALOUPE-PEACH CONSERVE

4 c. chopped cantaloupe	1/2 t nutmeg
4 c. chopped peaches	1/8 t salt
6 c. sugar	1 t grated orange
4 T lemon juice	peel
	1/2 c. walnuts

Mix the cantaloupe and peaches and bring to a boil. Add the sugar and lemon juice and cook until the conserve is thick. Add the nutmeg, salt, orange peel and walnuts. Cook for 3 minutes longer. Pour into hot jars and seal.

*

GREEN GRAPE MARMALADE

4 c. green grapes	4 c. sugar
1 c. water	Juice of 1 lemon

Simmer grapes in water until tender. Add sugar and boil to the jellying point, about 220 degrees. Add lemon juice and boil for 5 minutes longer.

*

GRAPE CATSUP

4 lbs. grapes   2 t cloves
2 lbs. sugar   2 t allspice
1 pt. vinegar   2 T cinnamon

Place grapes in pan and steam without water until soft. Put fruit through a sieve; add other ingredients and simmer mixture for 20 minutes. Seal in sterile, hot jars.

*

BEET JELLY

3 c. beet water   1 pkg. pectin
1 pkg. grape powdered   4 c. sugar
   drink mix

Beet water is obtained by cooking beets in it. Combine beet water, drink mix, and pectin. Mix well and bring to full boil. Add sugar and bring to boil again. Cook 1 minute. Pour into glasses and seal.

*

HONEY JELLY

3 c. honey   1/2 bottle fruit pectin
1 c. water

Bring honey and water to full rolling boil. Add pectin, stirring constantly. Boil 30 seconds. Remove from heat, skim, put into hot sterilized jars. Seal. Makes 5 - 6 cups.

*

WINE JELLY

3 c. sugar
2 c. Burgundy or fruit
  wine

1 T lemon juice
1/2 6-oz. bottle liquid
  pectin

In large saucepan, cook sugar, wine and lemon juice, keeping just below boiling point. Stir until sugar dissolves, about 5 minutes. Remove from heat. Stir in pectin. Skim off foam. Pour into clean, hot glasses. Makes 4 6-oz. glasses.

*

GREEN PEPPER JELLY

1 c. green pepper
6 c. sugar
1 1/2 c. vinegar

1 bottle pectin
Green food coloring

Cut peppers fine. Add sugar and vinegar and bring to boil. Add pectin. Stir in food coloring. Cool before pouring into jars.

*

APPLE SYRUP

1 c. cider
2 sticks cinnamon
12 cloves

1/8 t salt
1/2 c. brown sugar
2 T corn syrup

Combine cider with cinnamon, cloves, and salt. Simmer and strain. There should be 3/4 cup liquid. Combine with brown sugar and corn syrup. Boil 4 to 6 minutes. Serve as a syrup with pancakes.

*

PLUM SAUCE

1 1/2 lbs. plums
1 c. sugar
1/3 c. cider vinegar
1/3 c. horseradish

1/4 c. chopped onion
1 clove garlic, crushed
1 T salt

Combine all ingredients, bring to boil and simmer until plums are tender. Put in blender and puree (half the mixture at a time). Reheat, serve over spareribs, pork chops or broiled chicken.

*

PEAR SAUCE

4 pears
1/2 c. sugar
1/2 c. water
1/8 t salt

2 t lemon juice
1/2 t grated lemon rind
1/4 t vanilla extract

Peel, core and quarter pears. Cook in covered saucepan with sugar and water until pears are tender, about 30 minutes. Mash with remaining ingredients. Serve warm over gingerbread or ice cream.

*

The Great Lake State leads the Nation in growing plantation Christmas trees.

PEACH CHUTNEY

6 peaches
3/4 c. sugar
3/4 c. cider vinegar
1/4 t chopped garlic
1/2 c. water
1/3 c. cubed preserved
    ginger
2 T lemon juice
2 t curry powder

1 c. seedless raisins
1 1/2 t salt
1/4 t freshly ground
    black pepper
1/2 t red pepper
    flakes
5 ounces finely
    chopped onion

   Peel and pit peaches, cut each into eight
wedges. Heat sugar, vinegar, garlic and water
in saucepan. Stir until the sugar has dissolved.
Bring liquid to a boil and cook 5 minutes until
syrupy. Add peaches. Simmer 10 minutes. Remove peaches and reserve.
   Add remaining ingredients to the syrup.
Boil slowly for 10 minutes, or until mixture
thickens slightly. Return peaches to pan,
bring to a boil, then pour into a 1-quart
jar. Keep for a few days in the refrigerator
before serving. Makes 1 quart.

*

RHUBARB CHUTNEY

2 lbs. rhubarb
1 lb. golden raisins
1 lb. brown sugar
Juice of 3 lemons
4 cloves garlic, crushed

2 dried red chilies,
    chopped
1 t mustard seeds
1 T salt
1 pt. vinegar

   Wash, peel and dice the rhubarb. Combine
rest of ingredients in a heavy pan and bring
to a boil. Simmer 5 minutes for the flavors
to blend. Add rhubarb and cook very slowly
until chutney is thick, about 40 minutes.
Stir often. Pour into sterilized jars. Cover
well and keep at least one month before using.
Makes about 2 quarts.

*

BRANDIED CHERRIES

5 c. black cherries	2 c. sugar
2 1/2 c. water	1/2 c. brandy

Pit cherries. Cook pits in water 15 minutes. Measure out 2 cups liquid and pour in saucepan. Add sugar. Boil 5 minutes, stirring occasionally. Add cherries and cook 10 minutes. Remove cherries. Cook syrup until thick. Pour over cherries. Mix in brandy. Serve over ice cream, pudding or pound cake. Makes 2 pints.

*

HONEY SALAD DRESSING

1/2 c. cream, whipped	1 T honey
1 c. mayonnaise	1 t celery seed
1/4 t paprika	

Whip all ingredients together and cool. Serve over fruit salad.

*

CUCUMBER-BLUE CHEESE DRESSING

1 c. sour cream	1 T vinegar
1/2 c. crumbled blue cheese	1/4 t salt
	Dash pepper
1 1/2 T sugar	$\frac{1}{2}$ medium cucumber, shredded

Combine sour cream, blue cheese, sugar, vinegar, salt, and pepper. Stir in cucumber. Chill.

*

CINNAMON BUTTER

1/2 c. softened butter   1 T sugar
1 t lemon juice   1/2 t cinnamon

    Mix all ingredients together. Use as spread on muffins or quick breads.

*

CHEESE AND CHIVE BUTTER

1/2 c. softened butter   3 T shredded cheddar
1/2 t salt   cheese
1/8 t pepper   2 T chopped fresh
4 drops Tabasco   chives

    Mix all ingredients. Serve with corn on the cob, or on bread with sandwich meat.

*

DILL AND MUSTARD BUTTER

1/2 c. softened butter   1/2 t dill seed
1/2 t salt   1 t prepared
1/8 t pepper   mustard
4 drops Tabasco

    Mix all ingredients. Serve with corn on the cob, or on bread with sandwich meat.

*

soups
salads

PUMPKIN SOUP

2 c. diced, peeled and
  cleaned pumpkin
2 c. water
1 t salt
3 c. milk
1 c. evaporated milk

1 t sugar
6 slices dry bread,
  cubed
2 T butter
1 finely diced tomato

Bring pumpkin, salt and water to a boil. Then simmer 15 minutes. Drain and keep water. Mash pumpkin and stir back into water with milk, sugar, and bread. Return soup to boil. Simmer, covered, 10 minutes. Remove from heat and stir in butter and tomato slowly.

*

TURKEY CHEESE CHOWDER

1 c. finely chopped onion
1 c. finely chopped carrots
1 c. finely chopped celery
1/4 c. butter
1/4 c. flour
2 c. turkey or chicken
  broth

2 c. milk
1/4 t salt
1/8 t pepper
1 1/2 c. shredded
  cheese
2 c. diced cooked
  turkey

Saute chopped onions, carrots and celery in butter. Blend in flour. Gradually stir in broth, then milk. Cook, stirring constantly until mixture thickens. Stir in salt, pepper, cheese and turkey. Heat just until cheese melts. Do not boil. Serves 4.

*

CABBAGE SOUP

3 lbs. sliced cabbage
6 c. water
2 lbs. short ribs
1 t salt

1 medium onion,
  chopped
2 c. tomato sauce
3 T fresh lemon juice
2 t. brown sugar

Place cabbage in large Dutch oven. Add water, beef, salt and onion; heat to boiling. Reduce heat, cover and simmer for 2 hours. Stir in remaining ingredients. Cover and simmer 20 minutes more. Remove meat from pot. When cool enough to handle, cut meat from bones. Trim off fat. Cut meat into bite-size pieces and return to pot. Skim off any fat from soup. Makes about 12 cups.

*

CREAM OF MUSHROOM SOUP

1/2 lb. fresh mushrooms,
   sliced
1/2 c. onion, chopped
1/4 c. butter
2 c. chicken broth

3 c. milk
1 c. light cream
Dash of thyme
Salt and pepper to
   taste

Saute mushrooms and onion in butter. Add broth, milk, and cream. Season to taste with salt, pepper, and thyme. Serves 6.

*

ASPARAGUS SOUP

2 c. asparagus, cooked   1/16 t thyme
3 c. chicken or beef   1/8 t pepper
   stock

   Puree asparagus. Boil stock and combine with
thyme. Add pepper. Add asparagus and simmer five
minutes. Salt to taste. Makes 5 cups.

*

COLD MELON SOUP

1 cantaloupe   1/8 t cinnamon
4 T lemon juice   1/3 c. yogurt
2 t chopped mint   1/3 c. cream

   Peel and slice cantaloupe. Puree in blender
with lemon juice, mint and cinnamon. Chill. Stir
in yogurt and cream. Serves 4.

*

CHILLED STRAWBERRY SOUP

1 qt. strawberries   1/2 c. sugar
1/2 c. water   2 c. yogurt
1/2 c. orange juice

   Mix all ingredients in blender. Chill.
Serves 6.

*

OH, BEANS

by Judith A. Eldridge

Beans have probably been around about as long as politicians, or vice versa. Roman senators, as long ago as 2,000 years before Christ, used beans to cast their vote: a white bean for yes and a black one for no. Greeks, too, used beans for voting and jurors in those days cast their vote in trials with beans, white for innocent and black or red for guilty.

Even before that, Esau declared he'd sell his soul for a hot meal, and he did: translators of ancient scrolls called it a mess of pottage, but it was more likely a pot of beans.

Soldiers have known all about beans since wars were invented. For 1,500 years, Babylonian army rations were pork and beans, and that was long before Campbell's put them on the shelves for us civilians too.

Egyptians were eating beans back in the Bronze Age. When they weren't eating them, they used them in rituals to the dead. A Roman ritual held at midnight on the third and final day of Lemuria, an annual "entertainment" for the dead, called for the head of the household to walk barefoot through all the rooms of his house, casting black beans behind him and intoning nine times, "These I give and with these I redeem myself and my family." Ghosts supposedly followed close behind, picked up the beans and departed until the appointed time the next year.

OH, BEANS is an excerpt from the book with the same title by Judith A. Eldridge. Judy's book which has hundreds of bean recipes as well as interesting articles about Michigan's number one crop, is available for $5.65 ppd. from: Rowboat Features, 6148 N. Raindrop Road, East Lansing, MI 48823.

The Japanese have a similar ritual involving beans, luck and the New Year. At midnight on New Year's Eve, the head of the household dresses up in his (or her) richest garments and goes through every room, scattering roasted beans about and saying, "Out--demons! In--luck!"

As time progressed, people put aside such notions. They used beans for things like curing baldness. Mashed beans and garlic was a sure cure for coughs and colds in the Middle Ages, and witches used them in their magic brews to cast spells.

In the New World, thrifty New York farmers were growing beans as a cash crop. French settlers in Detroit shipped beans to Europe, for the first known export of beans--Michigan now ships thousands of tons of beans all over the world.

Navy beans reportedly got their name from Commodore Oliver Perry who is supposed to have coined the term while eating beans aboard ship in Lake Erie during the War of 1812. "Give me some more beans, navie," he probably shouted to the cook's helper.

Michigan got into the bean business when a doubting Thomas from Michigan, coming home from the Civil War by way of his cousins's farm in New York state, put a handful of beans in his pocket and said, according to legend, "I don't know if these'll grow back home or not, but...."

They did, and they do.

Back to the politicians. The story goes that in 1904, on a hot and humid summer day, Representative Joseph G. Cannon of Illinois came into the House restaurant and asked for bean soup, only to learn it had been taken from the menu.

"Thunderation!" he shouted, "I had my mouth set for bean soup. From now on, hot or cold, rain, or shine, I want it on the menu every day!'

And it has been.

In 1907, Senator Knute Nelson of Minnesota, perhaps jealous of the men in the other dining room, had it put on the Senate restaurant menu, too, by unanimous approval of the Rules Committee. He even furnished a Scandinavian recipe from his home state for it.

Then in the fall of 1975, a great bean scandal erupted. It was found, by a Michigan Representative from Saginaw, heart of the bean growing country, that the soup was being made with great northern beans from the Western states, rather than navy beans from Michigan. He was naturally upset.

It turned out that one year, when navies had been in short supply, someone had ordered great northerns and, since nobody ever complained, Michigan beans were never re-ordered.

The Congressman, of course, saw to it that something was done about that. Now both Senators and Representatives are again eating bean soup-- made with Michigan beans, of course.

*   *   *

Here's the recipe used in the Senate dining room, furnished by Chef James Lee:

THE FAMOUS SENATE RESTAURANT BEAN SOUP RECIPE

Take two pounds of small Michigan navy beans, wash, and run through hot water until beans are white again. Put on the fire with four quarts of hot water. Then take one and one-half pounds of smoked ham hocks, boil slowly approximately 3 hours in covered pot. Braise one onion chopped in a little butter, and when light brown, put in bean soup. Season with salt and pepper, then serve. Do not add salt until ready to serve. (Eight persons.)

*   *   *

And here's one used in the House:

U.S. HOUSE OF REPRESENTATIVES BEAN SOUP

2 lbs. Michigan navy beans   Salt and pepper
Smoked ham hock

    Cover beans with water and soak overnight.
Do not drain.   Add a smoked ham hock (and more
water to cover, if necessary.)   Simmer slowly for
about 4 hours until beans are tender; then add
salt and pepper to taste.   Just before serving,
bruise beans with large spoon or ladle, enough
to cloud.
    Makes 6 servings.

*

Pictured Rocks Nat'l Lakeshore, Lake Superior

The U.S. Navy, which serves beans daily, has sponsored contests for the best bean recipes from Navy cooks. Following are two recipes that took first and second places in the 1961 bean challenge.

S.S. McGINTY NAVY BEAN SOUP

1 1/2 c. Michigan navy beans
5 1/2 c. water
5 oz. diced pork sausage
3 T grated carrots
3 T chopped green onions
1 beef bouillon cube
1 T dehydrated potato
1/2 c. tomato soup, undiluted
1 1/2 t salt
1/2 t pepper
1 c. water
1 t Accent

Combine beans, water, sausage, carrots, onions and bouillion cube. Bring to boil, cover and reduce heat, simmer on low for 2 hours. Let cool 1 hour and drain, saving liquid. Grind or mash beans and pork, add to bean liquid with tomato soup, salt, pepper, potato granules mixed with the cup of water and Accent. Cook over low heat 30 minutes, stirring occassionally.

1st Prize, J.T. Ventura
Commissaryman 2nd Class
Destroyer Escort McGinty

ALAMEDA NAVY BEAN SOUP

1 c. Michigan navy beans
4 c. water
Split ham bone
1/2 c. chopped onion
2 medium carrots, chopped
2 ribs celery, chopped
Salt and pepper to taste
1/8 c. green pepper, minced
1/2 c. tomato puree
1/8 t prepared mustard
1 whole clove
2 peppercorns

Soak beans overnight in water to cover. Drain, combine all ingredients and simmer over low heat 4 hours, stirring and adding more liquid if necessary. Top with chopped parsley.

2nd Prize, W.C. Shireley
Chief Commissaryman
Alameda Naval Air Station, CA

8-LAYER SALAD

1 layer chopped lettuce
1 layer chopped spinach
1 layer chopped celery
1 layer chopped green
   pepper
1 layer chopped onion

1 layer cooked and
   drained, frozen green
   peas
1 layer mayonnaise,
   evenly spread
1 layer crushed crisp
   bacon bits

Use a large bowl. Add each layer to pan in order listed. Cover and store in refrigerator overnight.

*

RUBY SALAD

1/4 c. diced cooked beets
1/4 c. French dressing
1/4 c. diced celery

1/8 t salt
4 tomatoes
1 hard-boiled egg

Marinate beets in French dressing for 1 hour or more. Combine with celery and salt. Peel tomatoes, remove centers, and fill with beet mixture. Chop eggs finely and garnish over tomatoes in lettuce cups. Serve with Russian dressing. Serves 4.

*

TURKEY WALDORF SALAD

4 c. diced turkey
1 c. diced celery
2 c. diced apples

1/2 c. chopped walnuts
1 1/2 c. mayonnaise
1 T lemon juice

Mix all ingredients together. Chill and serve on lettuce leaves. Serves 6.

*

CUCUMBER GELATIN SALAD

1 pkg. lime gelatin   1/2 t salt
3 T lemon juice   2 c. diced cucumbers
1/2 c. mayonnaise

    Make gelatin as directed on package using
1/2 cup less water. Beat in remaining ingredients
except cucumbers. Freeze 20 minutes until soft
in center and firm at the edge. Whip until
fluffy. Fold in cucumbers. Pour into mold and
chill until firm. Serves 6-8.

*

HOT CABBAGE SALAD

4 slices bacon, diced   2 T vinegar
2 T chopped onion   2 T sugar
2 T chopped green   3 C chopped cabbage
  pepper

    In skillet cook bacon till crisp. Drain off
excess fat. To bacon add onion, green pepper,
vinegar and sugar. Heat through. Pour over
cabbage and toss.

*

PEACH RIDGE APPLE SMORGASBORD

The following recipe, as well as the ones for APPLE MUFFINS, DUTCH APPLE PIE AND APPLE CHERRY PIE, are from the Apple Smorgasbord held at the Hotel Statler in Detroit in 1955. The Smorgasbord was put on by the Michigan State Apple Commission and the International Apple Association. But let's not forget the women of Peach Ridge who helped out--Who? Where?

The wives of Peach Ridge (near Sparta in Western Michigan) growers put on apple smorgasbord for years, inviting food editors and other interested persons from around the country. A real down-home event, these women worked all year to get things ready for the second Tuesday in September each year. At that time, the family-tested dishes would turn up at the feast in the growers' yards. When everyone was sufficiently stuffed, it was time for dancing--square dancing was ex-Gov. G. Mennen Williams favorite at these affairs.

And these women knew how to plan--from using green table cloths for the food table (because it looked more colorful) and white for the eating ones. Their committees met year 'round to make sure every smorgasbord would be perfect.

"We sure got to know our neighbors," said Jo Reister, involved in it from the beginning in the 1950s until the end in the late 1970s. "But some people just thought it was too much work, so the project was abandoned."

Too bad. There's nothing wrong with a good down-home event.

CHICKEN APPLE SALAD

Combine:

1 small cooked chicken, diced	1/2 red pepper
3/4 c. celery, diced	Small bottle olives, drained
1 small can peas, drained	1 cup apple, diced
1 medium onion, diced	1/2 c. broken nutmeats

Toss together with salad dressing thinned with cream and 1 teaspoon mustard.

*

CAULIFLOWER SALAD

2 c. thinly sliced cauliflower	4 1/2 T salad or olive oil
1/2 c. chopped green olives	1 1/2 T lemon juice
1/3 c. finely chopped green pepper	1 1/2 T wine vinegar
3 T chopped onion	1 t salt
	1/4 t sugar
	Dash of pepper

In medium bowl, combine vegetables. Combine remaining ingredients in a small bowl and beat with rotary beater until well blended. Pour over vegetables and chill 1 hour. Serves 4.

*

ONION SALAD

2/3 c. water	3/4 t celery salt
1/2 c. vinegar	1 c. mayonnaise
3/4 c. sugar	Salt and pepper
2 t salt	Chives
6 onions, sliced	

Mix water with vinegar, sugar and salt. Bring to a boil and add onion slices. Marinate 3 to 4 hours, stirring occasionally. Drain and add celery salt and mayonnaise. Add salt and pepper to taste. Garnish with chives.

*

main dishes

BEEF SUPPER A LA MICHIGAN

2 lb. stew beef, cut in 1"
  cubes
Salt
Pepper
2 large onions, sliced
2 T oil
1 4½-oz. can whole
  mushrooms
4 medium potatoes, thinly
  sliced

1 10½-oz. can cream of
  mushroom soup
3/4 c. milk
3/4 c. sour cream
1 t salt
1/4 t pepper
2 c. shredded cheddar
  cheese

Season meat with salt and pepper. Cook and stir meat and onions in oil in large skillet over medium heat until meat is brown and onions are tender. Pour off oil. Drain mushrooms, reserving liquid. Add enough water to mushroom liquid to make 1 cup. Stir mushrooms and liquid into meat and onions. Heat to boiling, reduce heat and cover. Simmer 2 hours. Heat oven to 350 degrees. Pour meat mixture into 13x9-inch baking dish. Arrange potatoes over meat. Mix soup, milk, sour cream, salt and pepper; pour over potatoes. Sprinkle with cheese. Bake uncovered for 1 hour. Sprinkle with cracker crumbs if desired; bake uncovered until potatoes are tender and crumbs are brown, 20-30 minutes. Serves 8.

*

In Michigan you are never more than six miles from a lake or a stream.

OVEN SWISS STEAK

1 1/2 lbs. beef round steak, cut 3/4" thick
1/4 c. flour
1 1/2 t salt
2 T oil
1 16-oz. can tomatoes, cut up
1/2 c. finely chopped celery
1/2 c. finely chopped carrot
1/2 t Worcestershire sauce

Cut meat into 6 portions. Combine flour and salt. With meat mallet, pound 2 tablespoons of the mixture into meat on both sides. Brown meat on both sides in oil. Transfer meat to a 12x7½" baking dish. Blend remaining 2 tablespoons flour mixture into pan drippings. Stir in undrained tomatoes, celery, carrots and Worcestershire. Cook and stir till thickened and bubbly, pour over meat.

Bake steak, covered, at 350 degrees about 1 hour and 20 minutes or till meat is tender. Serves 6.

*

CHEESE STRATA

8 slices white bread
2 1/2 c. milk
4 eggs
1/2 lb. Cheddar cheese, cubed
1 t salt
1/2 t dry mustard
Dash pepper

Remove crusts from bread. Cut bread into 1" cubes and put in a greased 9x13" baking pan. In a blender or food processor, combine milk, eggs, cheese and seasonings. Pour over bread cubes, making sure all cubes are moistened. Cover and let stand overnight in refrigerator. Bake at 325 degrees for 1 hour. Serves 6.

*

CHEESE SOUFFLE

1/4 c. butter	1/2 lb. grated nippy Michigan
1/4 c. flour	cheese
1/2 t salt	4 egg yolks
1 c. milk	4 egg whites

Melt butter in top of double boiler. Add flour and salt and blend. Add milk slowly, stirring constantly. Cook until thick and smooth. Add cheese and cover. Let stand over boiling water until cheese is soft, then stir to blend. Beat egg yolks. Add 2 or 3 tablespoons of hot mixture to the egg yolks, stirring well. Then stir yolks into hot mixture slowly. Beat egg whites until stiff but not dry. Turn hot cheese mixture into a large bowl. Fold in whipped egg white until thoroughly combined and mixture is light and fluffy. Pour into ungreased casserole 2/3 full. Never cover. Place in 325 degree oven and bake 1 hour and 15 minutes. Do not open oven. Serve at once.

*

POPOVER CHICKEN

2 1/2 to 3 lb. broiler-
    fryer, cut up
	1 3-oz. can sliced
	    mushrooms, drained

3 eggs	1 T butter
1 1/2 c. milk	1 can condensed cream
1 1/2 c. flour	of mushroom soup
3/4 t salt	1/4 c. milk
1 T oil	
1 T fresh tarragon	

Brown chicken in 2 tablespoons cooking oil; season with a little salt and pepper. Place chicken in well-greased shallow 2-qt. baking dish. Combine eggs, milk, flour, and salt. Beat 1½ minutes. Add oil and tarragon; beat 30 seconds more. Pour over chicken. Bake at 350 degrees for 60 minutes. In saucepan, cook mushrooms in butter for 4 to 5 minutes. Add soup; gradually stir in the 1/4 c. milk, heat through. Serve sauce with chicken.

*

CHICKEN-POTATO BAKE

2 T butter
1/4 c. flour
1/2 t salt
1 broiler-fryer (about
   2 lb.-cut up)

4 medium-size potatoes,
   sliced
2 carrots, cut into 2"
   sticks
1 t salt
1 t tarragon

Melt butter in 13x9" baking pan in 375 degree oven. Combine flour and salt. Add chicken pieces, and coat with flour. Place skin side down in melted butter.

Bake chicken 20 minutes at 375 degrees. Remove from oven; place potatoes and carrots in bottom of pan, turning to coat with butter. Arrange chicken over vegetables, skin side up. Sprinkle salt and tarragon over all; cover.

Return to oven and bake 20 minutes more. Remove cover; baste with pan juices and bake at 400 degrees for remaining 20 minutes. Serves 4.

*

COTTAGE CHEESE-BEEF PIE

9" pie shell
1 lb. ground beef
1/2 c. chopped onions
1/4 c. canned brown
   gravy

1/2 t salt
Dash pepper
2 eggs
1 c. cottage cheese
Paprika

Brown meat and onions. Drain off fat. Add gravy and seasonings. Let mixture cool. Fill unbaked pie shell with mixture. Beat eggs and mix with cottage cheese. Spread cheese mixture over meat. Sprinkle paprika on top. Bake in a 350 degree oven for 30 minutes. Makes 6 to 8 servings.

*

STUFFED PUMPKIN

Pumpkins are fun, not only for kids, but cooks as well. They're inexpensive--especially if you grow your own (one package of seeds yields millions)-- and can be boiled down on a crispy fall day while you're puttering around the house. A 3 lb. one will give you about 3 lbs. of usable pumpkin--enough for 2-3 pies. To turn pumpkins into edible things, grab a large cleaver (electric knife or chain saw also works well) and split open. Clean out all the seeds and fiber. Cut into small pieces and peel. Cook in boiling water to cover 25-30 minutes, or until tender. Drain well and mash. Presto--it's ready to use. If you make too much, simply spoon into freezer containers, cool and freeze.

3 bacon strips
3 T chopped onion
2 T chopped celery
2 slices bread, cubed
1/2 t salt
1/8 t pepper
1 egg

1/3 c. milk
1/4 t allspice
3/4 lb. mild bulk
  sausage
1 t brown sugar
1 T vinegar
1 small pumpkin

Cut the top third of pumpkin off. Clean out pumpkin. Set pumpkin, cut side down, in a Dutch oven with ½" water. Boil water, cover and reduce heat to steam pumpkin until just tender, about 20-25 minutes.

Fry bacon till crisp. Remove bacon and saute onions and celery. Add bread, salt, and pepper, remove from heat and toss ingredients to mix. Beat egg in bowl. Stir in milk, allspice, bread mixture and crumbled bacon. In skillet, fry sausage until done. Drain well and stir into bread mixture.

Mix brown sugar with vinegar. Rub inside of pumpkin with brown sugar mixture. Spoon stuffing into pumpkin. Put foil over to cover and bake 40 minutes at 350 degrees. Remove foil and bake uncovered 20 minutes longer. Carve in half or quarters at table. Serves 2-4.

*

LAMB CABBAGE DINNER

1 lb. ground lamb
1 c. soft bread crumbs
1 egg
1/4 t garlic salt
1/4 t salt
1 T butter
1 envelope onion soup
   mix

1 c. water
3/4 t caraway seeds
3 c. coarsely chopped
   cabbage
1 c. sour cream
2 T flour

Mix lamb, bread crumbs, egg, garlic salt, and salt. Shape into 16 meatballs. Brown in butter and move to side of skillet.

Mix onion soup mix, water and caraway seeds. Add to skillet. Stir in cabbage. Heat to boiling. Reduce heat, cover and simmer 20 minutes.

Mix sour cream and flour. Skim excess fat from skillet. Stir few tablespoonfuls liquid from skillet into sour cream, return to skillet. Cook and stir over low heat until thickened and hot (do not boil). Serves 4.

*

EGGS IN THE HOLE

1 slice bread
1 egg

Butter
Salt and pepper to taste

Using a glass, cut the centers from the bread slice. Put bread slice in a skillet with about 3 tablespoons butter. Break egg into the hole in the bread. Cook over medium heat until egg is pretty well set. Add salt and pepper to taste. Turn egg over and cook another minute or two until done.

(Of course, you can make more than one at a time on a griddle by multiplying the recipe).

*

LEMON-GARLIC ROAST LAMB

1 leg of lamb (about
   5 lbs.)
1 T grated lemon peel
2 cloves garlic, peeled,
   finely chopped

1 t salt
1/4 c. pan drippings
1/4 c. flour
2 c. water
Salt and pepper

Place meat fat side up on rack in open shallow roasting pan.

Mix grated lemon peel with garlic and 1 teaspoon salt. Rub garlic mixture over surface of lamb.

Insert meat thermometer so tip is in thickest part of meat and does not touch bone or fat. Roast lamb until thermometer registers 175 degrees, about 3 hours at 325 degrees.

Remove lamb from pan and pour drippings from pan into bowl, leaving brown particles in pan. Return drippings (1/4 cup) to pan. Mix in flour. Cook over low heat, stirring until mixture is smooth. Remove from heat, stir in water. Heat to boiling, stirring constantly. Boil and stir 1 minutes. Season to taste. Serves 6.

*

Ironwood, Michigan, is as far west as St. Louis, Missouri; Port Huron is as far east as St. Petersburg, Florida; Hancock is farther north than Quebec City; Sturgis is farther south than Crescent City, California; and Windsor, Ontario, is actually south of Detroit.

BAKED SPARERIBS

4 lbs. spareribs
1 t onion salt
1 t celery salt
1/2 t garlic salt
1 t sage
1/2 t marjoram

Salt and pepper
Water
4 medium potatoes
8 small carrots
4 medium onions

Mix seasoning. Rub seasoning into meat. Place meat in roasting pan. Add 1 cup of water, cover, bake at 350 degrees about 1 hour.
Cut vegetables in half. Arrange around meat. Cover and bake 1 hour longer. Add more water if needed.

*

GRILLED MAPLE CHOPS

4 1" thick pork chops
Red wine
Salt and pepper
1/2 c. maple syrup

1/3 c. catsup
1 t garlic salt
1/2 t celery seed
1 t onion flakes

Marinate chops 4 hours in red wine. Sprinkle with salt and pepper on both sides. Combine remaining ingredients and baste while grilling.

*

EASY PORK ROAST

3 1/2 to 4 lbs. boneless pork loin, rolled and tied
Salt
1 T soy sauce
2 t crushed sage leaves
1/2 t pepper
1/2 t garlic salt
4 c. potatoes in 7" cubes

Place roast in baking dish. Combine 1/2 teaspoon salt and next 4 ingredients and rub into roast. Bake in 325 degree oven for 1 hour and 45 minutes.

Remove roast from oven. Arrange potatoes around meat, baste with pan drippings. Put back in oven and bake 30 minutes or until done. Remove string and cut meat into thin slices. Serves 8.

*

SAUERKRAUT-HOT DOG CASSEROLE

(Easy to make, disappears in a flash)

1 lbs. hot dogs, cut in 1" pieces
1 can cream of mushroom soup
1/2 c. mayonnaise
1 t caraway seeds
2 c. sauerkraut (drained)
4 c. diced cooked potatoes
1/2 c. buttered crumbs
Paprika

Mix together hot dogs, soup, mayonnaise, caraway seeds, sauerkraut and potatoes. Place in buttered casserole. Sprinkle with buttered crumbs and paprika. Bake at 350 degrees for 45 minutes. Serves 6.

*

BRAISED BEEF IN RED WINE

3 c. dry red wine
1 c. water
2 c. sliced onion
2 c. sliced carrots
2 cloves garlic,
  sliced
1/2 t thyme
1 t salt

1/2 t pepper
5-6 lb. pot roast
2 T oil
1 can beef broth
1 8-oz. can tomato sauce
3 T cornstarch
3 T water

Combine wine, water, onion, carrots, garlic thyme, salt and pepper for marinade. Place meat in bowl. Pour marinade over meat and refrigerate overnight. Remove meat from marinade; dry with paper towels. Reserve marinade. Heat oil in Dutch oven. Brown meat on all sides. Add marinade, beef broth and tomato sauce. Cover. Bring to boiling. Simmer for 2 1/2 to 3 hours or until meat is tender. Remove meat from pan. Skim all fat from sauce.

Mix cornstarch and water together. Heat with marinade mixture for gravy.

*

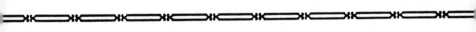

In 1879, Detroit telephone customers were first in the nation to be assigned phone numbers to facilitate handling calls.

Recipes abound for the REAL pasty. (I claim one on page 39 of MICHIGAN COOKING...AND OTHER THINGS). However, I found a pretty good fake one using turkey instead of beef. I suppose Cornish old-timers in the U.P. mines would sooner go without lunch than stuff one of these in their shirts in the morning, but here it is anyway.

TURKEY PASTIES

1 T flour
1 T sugar
1 t salt
1/4 t ground allspice
1/2 c. mayonnaise
1/2 c. sour cream

3 c. cut-up cooked turkey
3 c. diced apples
1/2 c. golden raisins
2 t parsley
2 pkgs. (11 ozs. each) pie
  crust mix

Measure flour, sugar, salt and allspice into large mixing bowl. Stir in mayonnaise and sour cream. Mix in turkey, apples, raisins and parsley.

Prepare pastry according to package directions. Divide dough from each package into 3 balls.

Roll each ball into 7-inch circle. Spoon 1 cup turkey mixture onto half the circle. Moisten edge of half the circle with water. Bring half over filling and pinch to seal. Place on ungreased baking sheet.

Bake at 400 degrees until pastry is golden brown, 35 to 40 minutes. Makes 6.

*

LUMBERJACKING IN ONTONAGON

by Bob Clock

Aside from birthdays, nothing makes a fellow feel older than remembering things other people have only read about in history books.

Take the lumber camps, for example. I don't carry a cane, yet, and I try not to say, "By cracky!", but I remember when at least one town in Michigan--Ontonagon in the Upper Peninsula-- was supported almost entirely by the lumber industry.

In fact, I worked for the Gorman Lumber Co. one summer as a section hand on the company-owned railroad. The line ran east from Ontonagon along the Lake Superior shore to bring in logs from the woods.

Judging from the reports of recent visitors, Ontonagon isn't half the town it used to be in its rip-roaring lumber heyday. When I worked there in 1948, the town had a population of 2,100 people. It was a matter of pride with the local citizenry that in an emergency, the entire population could be accommodated in its 21 bars without crowding. (To be truthful, one bar was closed while I was there for allowing nefarious activities in the booths, but that's another story).

The lumberjack was much in evidence on the streets of Ontonagon in those days, although only a fraction of the fellows working in the woods were ever in town at any one time. They would work

---

Bob Clock, wire service editor for the Petoskey News Review, lives with his wife, Judy, and four children in Charlevoix where he keeps busy--and warm--chopping wood for the wood stove in their living room. This article was originally written for the Charlevoix Courier, where he was editor (and my first boss), in 1966.

two or three weeks and then come into Ontonagon on the
train to live it up in the saloons for a few days.

There were stories about 'jacks who would hand over
big bank rolls to their favorite bartenders and tell them
to let them know when they had drunk it up. There was
one bar which allegedly had a chute in the back room
leading to the basement. Gin-soaked 'jacks were dropped
down the chute where they slept it off in the basement
on mattresses supplied by the management. There were
lots of stories about 'jacks, and I believed every one
of them.

The shanghaiing of lumber jacks by logging camp
operators was accepted as a matter of course. Sunday
morning after a busy Saturday night the pickings were
particularly good. A dozen or more lumberjacks would
be sprawled along the walk in front of the Holly Hotel.
I knew one logging camp operator who would come into
town every Sabbath morn with his pickup truck. He
would survey the wreckage of the night before lying
on the sidewalk, select five or six strapping specimens, hoist them into the truck and off he'd go into
the woods.

Once sober, the 'jacks worked just long enough to
finance another binge in town. The system was so well
established I never heard one word against it, not
even from the lumberjacks themselves. Many, undoubt-
edly, were aggreeably surprised to wake up and find
themselves still in Ontonagon County rather than some
far corner of Hell.

The job of section hand is not the easiest in the
world, but there's no better way for a young fellow to
keep in shape. My first day on the job was spent
tamping railroad ties. Gandy dancing, we called it.
I don't think I've ever been so tired in my life.
Then, to make matters worse, I Gandy danced all that
night in my dreams. By morning I was ready for the
scrap heap.

After a while, the work, like most work, became
routine, but it was a pleasant routine. We'd leave
town at 7 a.m. every morning aboard our little gasoline

powered speeder. Before we reached the village
limits we would startle a doe or two browsing along
our right-of-way. Sometimes they'd lope along in
front of us for a while before striking off into
the woods.

Before long we'd be rumbling over the Flint
Steel River trestle. If we were lucky there'd be
a buck standing knee deep in the river, drinking.
When he'd hear the speeder he'd take off at a lazy
gallop through the marsh grass along the river, his
wet flanks glistening in the morning sun. Beyond
lay all of Lake Superior, cold and blue.

I don't believe it is generally known that
section hands developed a very excellent dietary
tradition over the years. They eat lunch twice,
once at 9 a.m. and again at noon. My first day on
the job, the 9 a.m. lunch break came as a complete
surprise. I downed both the Spam sandwiches I
had packed, along with a thermos of hot tea. I was
equally surprised, but also chagrined, when, at
noon, we knocked off for the main lunch hour and I
had nothing left to eat. Thereafter I packed two
lunches and I never ceased to be amazed at how
hungry a fellow can get by 9 o'clock in the morning
after a hearty breakfast.

As soon as we finished lunch, little Boris Kos-
lovitch, our Russian-born foreman who spoke only
fragmentary English, would rise slowly to his
feet, burp, and start walking slowly down the track,
head bowed and hands clasped behind his back. He
suffered from ulcers and had an idea walking
helped his digestion. He always carried a piece of
chalk with him to mark rotten cross - ties for re-
placement, so his therapy wasn't an entire waste
of time.

As soon as he'd leave, the young fellows in
the gang would high-tail it for the Lake Superior
shore. There wasn't a house or a cottage for miles
and miles in either direction and we had the beach
entirely to ourselves. I don't think the water
temperature ever crept out of the 40's that summer,

but after the first five minutes we'd be so completely numb we didn't notice how much it hurt.

Some days we were lucky enough to stop close to one of the huge sand pits found along the shore. They were six to eight feet deep and the water in them was tepid from the sun. You could make a deep dive right from the bank. No one knew how the pits got there, but I have heard since that Indians who inhabited those parts used to dig trenches along the shore to lay in ambush for their enemies.

Two of my co-workers on the section were John Balcom and Oscar Peterson, former lumberjacks who, in the winter of their lives, preferred to spend their evenings in town rather than in the woods. Both John and Oscar were remarkable in that they both remembered Paul Bunyan quite vividly and on rainy days they would regale us with stories of old Paul's legendary prowess. But that's another story in itself.

*   *   *

fish & game

THE WILY WOLVERINE

The nickname "Wolverine State" iden-
tifying the State of Michigan has,
for its origin, a practically extinct
mammal that once roamed its northern
forests...the crafty, fearless
wolverine.

Try to visualise an offspring fathered by a bear
and mothered by a skunk, and designed by a committee
and you will have some idea of this squat, lumbering
shaggy member of the weasel family -- the wolverine.
The wolverine is tough enough to outfight a full-
sized bruin, and ill-scented enough to make a skunk
turn up his nose. He has sometimes been called "The
Skunk Bear". He is an unsocial beastie, a lone
hunter, and so ill-tempered that he has been ostra-
cized by other members of the animal world because
of his downright meanness and unpleasant aroma. He
is extremely muscular and his movement is marked by

a rolling progress like a sailor fresh from a pitching deck. His body is covered with dark brown hair that is coarse and thick. He has feet like a bear with a hair covering that hides vicious braces of claws. His length, from pointed nose to the end of a bushy tail, runs from three to four feet. He is the largest of the American family of weasels.

A wolverine's temper is always the same.... ornery. His personality is about as mild as a prizefighter at the sound of the bell. He has been know to throw larger animals than himself, with a reputation for ferocity, into a state of fear, making them leave their kill, and then consuming the food himself. A real tough guy! His anger has a very short fuse. One of the things that will send him off into a murderous fury is to observe another animal enjoying a meal. His eyes snap, the hair stands up on his neck, his tail hoists and he tears forward to engage the unsuspecting diner in combat.

Victor H. Calahane, in his book, "Mammals of North America," tells of an instance where two adult black bears decided to beat a hasty retreat when a wolverine suddenly appeared and demanded their dinner. In another instance, two mountain lions, slunk away from a tasty repast when challenged by a snarling wolverine in California. One of the lions protested violently but was afraid to engage the bow-legged little robber.

The wolverine seems to have a perennial penchant for murder. Records show where he has attacked moose, caribou, sheep, deer, coyotes, bears and mountain lions. As his short legs and bear-like gait prevent him from chasing larger and faster animals successfully, he resorts to various stratagems. Hunters and trappers tell of his leaping upon elk and moose when they are bogged down in deep snow. The animals have been found with holes torn in their backs, their spinal cords

cut, and tracks leading away from the kill identify the
assassin...the wolverine. In some areas there is evidence
that the wolverine hunts sheep; sometimes following them
to the edge of a cliff or up a ravine, then making a
quick leap on to their backs and cutting their jugular
veins.

Here is a rebel of the forest that is the strongest
for its size of all North American mammals. He's ready
to defy and spit in the eye of animals many times his
size. Surprisingly, there are no reports of a wolverine ever attacking man.

And why all these killings? Because the wolverine
is a 14-carat glutton. He has an immense appetite,
consuming great quantities of food. His diet is varied.
He likes meat of all kinds and condition, from snails
and frogs to sheep and deer.

But the most interesting facet of the wolverine's
personality is its craftiness, a capacity to confound
man. For example, should he decide to follow a trap-
line, he may drive the poor trapper crazy and ultimately
ruin him. With diabolical ingenuity, he will remove
bait from traps, every trapped animal, and often hide
the traps or destroy them--and never get caught himself.

He is physically equipped by tooth and claw to
dig, climb or gnaw his way into almost any building. He
has broken into cabins and eaten or destroyed a whole
winter's cache of supplies in one week. Canned goods,
pots, pans, dishes, cutlery and even the kitchen stove
may be scattered throughout the woods as if out of
sheer deviltry. Flour or other food he doesn't care
to eat is spoiled by his vile smelling secretion.

Hunting and eating is such a happy occupation that
the wolverine will have no part of slothful hibernation
as followed by bears. On through the winter he con-
tinues his program of hunting, killing and eating
without interruption.

The wolverine is so secretive and elusive about
his living habits that little has been discovered
about his private life. He seems to be a solitary
grumpy fellow that seldom teams up with any other
animal, not even his own kind. An exception occurs

in February or March when he feels an urge to take
a mate. But the courtship is short, the honeymoon
soon over and he returns to the solitary life.

The fur coat of the wolverine is too bulky and
coarse to be useful for garments --pelts have little
dollar value. Eskimos do use his fur for trimming
their arctic space-suits and like it especially
around the edges of their parkas since wolverine
fur does not gather frost.

The wolverine has never been numerous in
this country and is now considered extinct east
of the Rockies. Only a small number are believed
to still roam the Rocky Mountains and the Sierra
Nevadas. Some specimens can still be seen in zoos
of our major cities.

* * *

RAINBOW TROUT WITH MUSHROOM STUFFING

6 pan-dressed rainbow
   trout (about 8 oz.
   each)
1 1/2 t salt

1/4 t pepper
Mushroom stuffing
2 T melted butter

Clean, wash and dry fish. Sprinkle inside and outside with salt and pepper. Place fish on well-greased pan. Stuff fish with Mushroom Stuffing. Brush with melted butter. Bake in 350 degree oven 25 to 30 minutes or until fish flakes easily when tested with a fork. Serves 6.

MUSHROOM STUFFING

1/2 lb. mushrooms,
   sliced
1 large onion, chopped
2 stalks celery,
   chopped
1/2 c. butter

1/4 c. finely chopped
   parsley
1 t thyme leaves
1/2 t salt
2 c. soft bread crumbs

Cook mushrooms, onion and celery in butter until tender. Remove from heat and toss with parsley, thyme, salt and bread crumbs.

*

Isle Royale National Park, located in Lake Superior, shelters the largest moose herd remaining in the United States.

BROILED SALMON

2 lbs. salmon steaks	1/2 t salt
3 T lemon juice	1/8 t pepper
1 t grated lemon rind	1/4 t marjoram
1/4 c. salad oil	1 T finely chopped onion

Place steaks in greased broiler pan, pour remaining ingredients over. Marinate steaks 20 minutes, turning at 10 minutes. Broil 5 minutes on each side, if steaks are 1 inch thick.

*

BAKED WHITEFISH WITH SOUR CREAM

1 4-lb. whitefish, split and de-boned	Paprika
2 c. sour cream	Butter

Flatten fish, rub inside and out with paprika and butter. Place in casserole and cover with sour cream.

Cover dish and bake about 45 minutes at 350 degrees.

*

PICKLED SMELT

Smelt	2 1/2 c. white sugar
Salt Water	10 small onions, sliced thin
1 qt. white vinegar	
1 c. or 1 pkg. mixed pickling spices	2 lemons, sliced

Wash smelt twice in water. Clip off heads, tails and fins. Soak fish in salt water (to float an egg) for 24 hours. Rinse.

Bring vinegar and sugar to a boil. Remove from heat, add onions and spices. Let cool. Pack fish into jars and cover with vinegar mixture, making sure onions and spices are evenly distributed. Put two slices of lemon in each jar and seal. Brine is enough for 10 pints.

SHERRY BAKED PARTRIDGE

2 partridges
1 clove of garlic,
  minced
1/2 small onion,
  chopped
1/3 c. butter

1 T celery, chopped
1/4 t pepper
1 t salt
3/4 c. sherry

Cut up birds, using breasts and thighs. Brown lightly with onion and garlic in butter. Put in roasting pan, add celery, salt and pepper and sherry. Bake 1 1/2 hours, covered, at 350 degrees, basting frequently and adding water if necessary.

*

BUNNY IN A BAG

1 or 2 rabbits, cut into
  serving pieces
1/4 c. flour
1 t salt
1/2 t pepper

1 onion, sliced
1 stalk celery, sliced
1 t soy sauce
2 T butter
3/4 c. dry red wine

Shake flour, salt and pepper in a 10x16" oven cooking bag and place into a roasting pan. Add rabbit and shake to coat the meat; then arrange the pieces around so they are on the bottom of the bag, in contact with the pan. Add onion, celery, butter, soy sauce, and wine. Secure bag with tie and make 6 slits on top. Bake 1 hour, until tender, in a 350 degree oven.

*

SQUIRREL FRICASSEE

1 large squirrel, cut
in serving pieces
3/4 c. flour
1/2 t salt
1/4 t pepper
4 slices bacon, chopped
fine

1 small onion, chopped
fine
2 t lemon juice
1 large apple, cored and
diced
1 1/2 c. chicken stock

Mix together flour and seasonings. Roll meat
in the mixture and coat evenly. Fry bacon; remove
and reserve it. Turn up heat and brown the meat
in the bacon fat. Sprinkle with onion and the
lemon juice. Return bacon to the skillet and add
apple and stock. Cover and simmer about 2 hours
until tender. Serves 4.

*

VENISON MINCEMEAT

2 lbs. cooked and ground
venison
4 lbs. chopped apple
2 lbs. raisins
4 c. brown sugar
3/4 lb. butter
1/2 lb. currants

1/2 t cloves
1 t allspice
1/2 t nutmeg
2 t salt
1 1/2 t cinnamon
1 lemon, ground

Add cider to cover mixture. Cook very
slowly until the fruits are tender (about 1
hour). This will keep indefinitely if put in
fruit jars or frozen.

*

PHEASANT AND SAUERKRAUT

1 pheasant
Butter

1 2 lb. can sauerkraut
1 apple, cored and quartered

Rub the bird with butter and brown under the broiler, about 10 minutes. Put in foil with the sauerkraut and apple. Seal foil and continue baking in a 325 degree oven for 1 1/2 hours.

*

POT ROAST OF BEAR SURPRISE

The surprise is that anyone would eat this.

Salt and pepper chuck of bear meat. Place in roasting pan. Add 1" hot water and 1/4 cup melted bear fat. Roast (covered) at 450 degrees, basting every 15 minutes until tender (2 to 4 hours).
Remove from roaster. Stir in flour, salt, pepper, and hot water for gravy.

(For another taste treat along this line, see Roast Bear Paws, page 56, in MICHIGAN COOKING... AND OTHER THINGS.)

*

vegetables

ASPARAGUS QUICHE

Pastry for one-crust 9"
  pie
3/4 lb. fresh asparagus
3 beaten eggs

1 1/2 c. light cream or
  milk
3/4 t salt
Dash nutmeg
1 1/2 c. shredded Swiss
  cheese

Bake shell at 450 degrees for 5 minutes. Meanwhile cook cut asparagus in boiling water 5 minutes. Beat together eggs, cream, salt and nutmeg. Put asparagus in pastry, pour egg mixture over. Top with Swiss cheese. Bake at 350 degrees for 1 hour or until brown on top.

*

SWEET 'N SOUR GREEN BEANS AND CELERY

1 lb. green beans
1 c. sliced celery,
  ¼" pieces
1/8 t pepper
2 T sugar

1 T cornstarch
1/4 t dry mustard
3 T vinegar
1 T chopped pimento

Wash beans and remove ends. Boil beans, celery and pepper in 1 inch salted water in 3-qt. saucepan. Simmer covered until beans are tender, about 15 minutes. Remove beans and celery.
Measure 1 cup bean liquid back into saucepan. Mix sugar, cornstarch and mustard; stir in vinegar and pimento. Stir into hot bean liquid. Cook and stir over medium-high heat until thick and bubbly. Stir vegetables into sauce. Serves 4.

*

DILLED GREEN BEANS

2 T chopped onion
1/4 c. chopped green
  pepper
1/2 t dill seed

1 c. beef broth
3 c. green beans,
  cut

Cook onion, pepper, dill seed, broth, and green beans about 25 minutes, or until beans are tender. Serves 6.

*

BLUE RIBBON BAKED CABBAGE

1 medium size head of
  cabbage, shredded
1 T sugar
2 T flour

1 c. cream
6 slices bacon
Salt and pepper to
  taste

Place shredded cabbage in casserole. Mix sugar and flour. Combine with cream, salt and pepper. Pour over cabbage. Cover cabbage with slices of bacon and bake 40 minutes at 350 degrees in a covered dish. Remove cover for a few minutes to crisp the bacon. Serves 6.

*

HONEY-BAKED ONIONS

1/3 c. honey
1/4 c. butter

1/2 t salt
6 large onions, sliced

Melt butter with honey and salt. Preheat oven to 425 degrees.
In greased 9x13" baking dish, arrange onion slices, pour mixture over onions. Bake 45 minutes or until golden. Serves 6.

*

CARROT SOUFFLE

4 eggs, separated	1/4 c. red wine
1/2 c. sugar	2 T lemon juice
1 c. grated raw carrots	1/2 t grated lemon rind
1/4 c. shredded apple	1/3 c. flour

Beat egg yolks with sugar until light and lemon-colored. Add carrots, apple, wine, lemon juice, lemon rind and flour; blend well. Beat egg whites until stiff peaks form; fold into carrot mixture. Spoon mixture into a well greased 1½ quart casserole. Bake at 375 degrees 35 to 40 minutes, until golden brown. Serve immediately. Serves 6.

*

CAULIFLOWER-CARROT CHEESE PIE

2 c. herb croutons, finely crushed	4 c. cauliflower flowerets
1/4 c. melted butter	1/2 c. sliced carrots
1 c. chopped onion	3/4 c. shredded Cheddar cheese
1 clove garlic	2 eggs
2 T butter	1/4 c. milk
1/4 t salt	3/4 c. shredded Cheddar cheese

Mix croutons and 1/4 c. butter. Press into a 9" pie pan. Bake at 375 degrees for 10 minutes. Cook onion and garlic in butter. Add salt. Stir in cauliflower and carrots. Cook, covered, for 10-15 minutes, or until vegetables are tender-crisp. Sprinkle 3/4 cup cheese on bottom of pie shell. Spoon vegetables on top. Mix eggs and milk, pour over vegetables. Bake at 375 degrees 15 minutes. Top with remaining cheese and bake 10 minutes more, or until set. Serves 8.

*

CELERY AND TOMATOES

1/4 c. butter
1 medium onion, chopped
1 16-oz. can tomatoes
1/2 t Tabasco

1/4 t thyme
4 c. cut celery
1 10-oz. pkg. frozen
   peas

    Melt butter in a large skillet and cook the onion until tender. Drain the tomatoes reserving the liquid; combine liquid with onions in skillet. Add Tabasco and thyme.
    Bring to a boil and stir in the celery and peas. Cover and cook 10 minutes, or until barely tender. Add the tomatoes, heat through and serve. Serves 8.

*

COOKOUT CORN

What's better than a cookout on the shores of Lake Michigan -- the waves rolling, the seagulls calling, your sunburn tingling? Of course, it wouldn't be complete without a toasty, golden brown fresh roasted ear of Michigan corn.

    Pull back the husks and remove the silks from fresh medium corn. Soak the cobs, husks and all, in cold water for 20 to 30 minutes. Drain the cobs, dry and brush with melted butter. Tie the husks back in place. Roll each cob up in a piece of aluminum foil, sealing it tightly. Place in the glowing coals of bonfire and let it roast, turning several times, for 20 to 30 minutes, depending on the size of the cob. Shuck the corn, add salt and pepper and more melted butter if desired. Get the next round ready.

*

CORN AND TOMATOES

2 c. corn
1/4 c. butter
1/4 c. chopped onion
1/4 c. chopped green
   pepper

2 t brown sugar
1/2 t salt
2 large tomatoes,
   cut up

Cook and stir all ingredients except the tomatoes over medium heat until the butter is melted. Cover, simmer 10 minutes.
Stir in the tomatoes. Cover, cook 5 minutes longer. Serves 4-6.

*

MUSHROOM CASSEROLE

1 lb. mushrooms
Butter
1 c. seasoned croutons
1/2 c. chopped onion
1/2 c. chopped celery

1/2 c. green pepper
1/2 c. mayonnaise
Salt and pepper to
   taste
1 can cream of mushroom
   soup

Saute coarsely chopped mushrooms in butter. In a casserole, place 1/2 cup croutons. Combine mushrooms with onion, celery, pepper, mayonnaise, salt, and pepper. Pour mixture over croutons.
Cover mushrooms with remaining croutons. Refrigerate overnight. Spoon undiluted mushroom soup over top. Insert knife so soup can go down into mixture. Cover and bake for 50-60 minutes at 300 degrees.

*

MUSHROOMS IN WINE

2 lb. mushrooms, sliced   1 t salt
1/3 c. oil   6 drops Tabasco
2 T chopped chives   3/4 c. dry white wine
1/3 c. chopped parsley

    Saute mushrooms in oil with chives and parsley.
Season with salt and Tabasco. Add wine. Cook over
low heat for 3 minutes. Serves 4-6.

*

TOMATO-ONIONS

2 c. water
1/2 t salt   1/4 c. chopped green pepper
12 small white onions,   1/4 c. chopped celery
   peeled   1/2 t salt
2 T butter   1/2 t basil leaves,
1 c. peeled chopped   crushed
   tomato

    Heat water and salt in skillet to boiling. Add
onions. Reduce heat, simmer covered until onions
are tender, about 15 minutes. Drain onions and
return to skillet.
    Add butter to onions, heat until melted. Stir
in tomato, green pepper, celery, salt and basil.
Heat to boiling. Reduce heat, cover and simmer
5 minutes. Serves 4.

*

CHEESY BAKED MASHED POTATOES

3 c. mashed potatoes
2 T flour
1 1/2 t salt
1/2 c. sour cream

1 T chopped chives
1 egg, slightly beaten
1/2 c. shredded Swiss
   cheese
4 slices bacon, crumbled

Mix potatoes, flour, and salt together. Spoon into greased 9x9-inch pan, spreading mixture to edges. Mix sour cream, chives and egg together, spread over potato mixture. Sprinkle cheese and bacon on top. Bake at 350 degrees for 25 to 30 minutes or until set. Cut into squares. Serves 4.

*

HASH BROWNS

4 medium potatoes
1 T finely chopped onion

1 t salt
Shortening

Peel and grate potatoes. Mix with onion and salt. Drop potatoes (4" patties) from spatula into shortening on griddle. Start on high heat, lower to medium to cook inside. Turn after 10 minutes. Cook until golden brown, about 10 minutes.

*

The Michigan State Fair was the first state fair in the United States.

BAKED STUFFED TOMATOES

8 large tomatoes,
   peeled
4 T butter
1/2 c. finely chopped
   onions
3 T flour
1 1/2 c. milk
1 t salt
1/4 t pepper

1/8 t thyme
1/8 t dry mustard
1/4 t Worcestershire sauce
1 c. grated Cheddar cheese
1 c. soft breadcrumbs

Cut a slice off top of tomatoes and scoop out the center pulp. Turn the tomatoes upside down to drain.

Saute the onion in butter. Blend in flour, add milk and seasonings and cook, stirring until thick. Add cheese and half the crumbs.

Arrange the tomatoes in a baking dish, fill them with the sauce and sprinkle remaining crumbs over them.

Bake at 375 degrees for 20 minutes.

*

ZUCCHINI CHEESE CASSEROLE

3 medium zucchini squash,
   sliced
1/2 c. chopped onion
2 T oil
1 lb. cottage cheese
1 t basil

1/2 t oregano
1/4 t salt
2 fresh tomatoes, peeled
   and sliced
1/3 c. grated Parmesan
   cheese

Saute zucchini and chopped onion in oil. Beat cottage cheese with basil, oregano, and salt. Place alternating layers of zucchini, cottage cheese and tomato in a 2-quart casserole dish. Top with Parmesan cheese. Bake at 350 degrees, uncovered, for 25 to 30 minutes.

Serves 6.

*

APPLESAUCE SQUASH

Halve acorn squash, remove seeds, bake 30 minutes at 350 degrees cut side down. Turn right side up. Fill with applesauce. Top with 1 t brown sugar, 1 t butter, and dash of cinnamon. Bake another 30 minutes.

*

CORN AND SOUR CREAM SQUASH

2 acorn squash
1 1/2 c. corn
2 T butter

Sour cream
2 slices bacon, crisp-
cooked, and crumbled

Halve squash and scoop out seeds. Bake squash cut side down in 350 degree oven for 30 minutes. Turn squash. Bake, covered with foil, for 20 to 30 minutes more or till tender.

Meanwhile, cook corn about 5 minutes or till tender. Drain. Toss with butter.

Spoon corn into squash centers. Top with sour cream and some of the crumbled bacon.

Serves 4.

*

Stand anywhere in Michigan and you are within 85 miles of one of the Great Lakes.

FRIED GREEN TOMATOES

4 medium-size green tomatoes	2 T butter
1/4 c. flour	2 T salad oil
1/4 c. yellow cornmeal	1/4 c. milk
1/2 t seasoned salt	1/4 c. dairy sour cream
1/8 t pepper	Fresh snipped dill or dill weed

Slice tomatoes 1/4" thick. Mix flour, cornmeal, salt, and pepper in a small bowl. Heat butter and oil in large skillet. Dip tomato slices into milk, then into cornmeal mixture.

Fry over medium heat until golden brown, about 3 minutes on each side. (Add more oil if necessary.) Top with a tablespoon of sour cream, sprinkle with dill.

Serves 4.

*

Old Mariner's Church, Detroit

Little Pt. Sable Lighthouse

breads
pancakes

APPLE MUFFINS WITH CRUNCH TOPPING

2 c. sifted flour	3/4 c. milk
3 t baking powder	1 c. chopped peeled
1/2 c. sugar	apple
1/2 t salt	1/3 c. brown sugar
3 T shortening	1/2 t cinnamon
1 egg, beaten	1/3 c. chopped walnuts

Sift together dry ingredients. Cut in shortening. Combine egg and milk. Add to flour mixture; mix until flour is just dampened. Fold in apple. Fill muffin tins 1/2 full. Combine brown sugar, cinnamon and nuts. Sprinkle over batter. Bake at 400 degrees for 25 minutes. Makes 12 muffins.

*

CORN BREAD

1 c. flour	1 c. yellow corn meal
1/4 c. sugar	2 eggs
4 t baking powder	1 c. milk
1 t salt	1/4 c. shortening

Blend dry ingredients well. Add remaining ingredients and beat until smooth, about 1 minute. Pour into greased 9x9-inch pan and bake at 425 degrees for 20-25 minutes.

*

CHERRY KUCHEN

1 egg, beaten well
1/2 c. sugar
1/4 c. milk
1/2 t vanilla
1 1/2 c. biscuit mix
1 1/2 c. drained and
   chopped red cherries

1/4 c. flour
1/2 c. brown sugar
1/2 t cinnamon
3 T butter
1/4 c. nuts, chopped

Combine beaten egg, sugar, milk and vanilla. Add biscuit mix and stir until smooth. Pour into a greased 8x8-inch pan. Sprinkle drained chopped cherries evenly over batter. Mix flour, brown sugar and cinnamon well; cut in butter until like cornmeal, add nuts and sprinkle over cherries. Bake at 375 degrees about 30 minutes. Serve as coffee cake or covered with cream. Serves 9.

*

OATMEAL PANCAKES

3/4 c. quick oatmeal,
   cooked according to
   pkg. directions
1 1/2 c. milk
1 egg

2 T honey
2 T oil
1 c. flour
1 1/2 t baking powder
1/2 t salt

Cool cooked oatmeal. Add milk, egg, honey, oil and stir well. Sift dry ingredients together and stir into batter. Fry on lightly greased griddle until golden brown on each side.

*

PEAR BREAD

1/2 c. butter	1 t baking powder
1 c. sugar	1/8 t nutmeg
2 eggs	1/4 c. sour cream
2 c. flour	1 c. coarsely chopped,
1/2 t salt	cored pears
1/2 t baking soda	1 t vanilla

Cream butter and sugar. Beat in eggs one at a time. Combine dry ingredients, add to egg mixture. Mix in sour cream. Stir in pears and vanilla. Pour into buttered 9"x5" loaf pan. Bake at 350 degrees for 1 hour.

*

BRAN-APPLE COFFEE CAKE

3 1/2 c. flour	1 1/2 c. sugar
1/2 c. packed brown	1/3 c. butter
sugar	2 eggs
1 t ground cinnamon	1 c. buttermilk
1/2 c. butter	1 c. applesauce
3 c. whole bran cereal	2 1/2 t baking soda
1 c. boiling water	1/2 t salt

Combine 1 cup flour, brown sugar and cinnamon. Cut in the 1/2 cup butter. Set aside. Combine 1 cup of the cereal with 1 cup boiling water, set aside. Cream the sugar and the 1/3 cup butter. Beat in eggs. Mix in milk, applesauce, and bran. Combine the remaining flour, soda and 1/2 teaspoon salt. Add the remaining cereal and egg mixture, blend well. Pour into two greased 9x9x2-" baking pans. Sprinkle half of the cinnamon mixture over each. Bake in 400 degree oven for 30 to 35 minutes. Makes 2 coffee cakes.

*

CORN FRITTERS

When I was an elementary student at Greenfield Village in the 1950s, one of my winter-time favorites at lunch in the Clinton Inn was piping hot corn fritters with maple syrup. This recipe is as close as I can get to duplicating that treat.

6 ears corn	2 t baking powder
Milk	1/2 t salt
1 1/2 c. flour	1 egg, beaten

Cut 2 cups corn off cobs and drain, reserving liquid. Add enough milk to make 1 cup. Sift dry ingredients. Mix egg with milk mixture and corn. Add to dry ingredients, mixing just till moist.

Drop batter by tablespoon into hot oil (375 degrees). Fry until golden brown, 2-3 minutes. Drain on paper towels. Serve with hot maple syrup. Makes about 16.

*

Scotch Settlement School, Greenfield Village

PLUM MUFFINS

3/4 lb. plums, finely
  chopped
2 1/2 c. flour
2 t baking soda
1/2 t salt
1 c. sugar

1/4 c. butter, melted
2 eggs, slightly beaten
1/2 c. milk
1/2 c. chopped walnuts
1 T sugar

Preheat oven to 400 degrees.
Sprinkle plums with 1 tablespoon flour and toss lightly. In a large bowl combine flour, baking soda and salt with 1 cup sugar. In another bowl combine melted butter, eggs, and milk, stir until smooth. Add the liquid ingredients to dry ingredients. Stir just until mixture is moistened. Fold in plums and walnuts. Spoon batter into muffin cups, filling about 2/3 full. Sprinkle remaining tablespoon of sugar on top of batter.
Bake 20 to 25 minutes. Serves 18.

*

Holland Tulip Fields

HERB BREAD

1 1/4 c. warm water	3 c. flour
1 pkg. dry yeast	1/2 t nutmeg
2 T shortening	1 t sage
2 t salt	2 t caraway seeds
2 T sugar	

In mixer bowl, dissolve yeast in warm water. Add shortening, salt, sugar, half of flour. Beat 2 minutes. Add remaining flour, nutmeg, sage, caraway seeds and blend in with spoon until smooth. Scrape batter from sides of bowl. Cover with cloth, let rise in a warm place until double (about 30 minutes).

Stir down by beating about 25 strokes. Spread batter evenly in greased loaf pan 9"x5"x3". Batter will be sticky. Smooth out top of loaf by flouring hand and patting into shape.

Let rise in warm place until batter reaches 1" from top of pan (about 40 minutes).

Heat oven to 375 degrees. Bake 45 to 50 minutes or until brown. Immediately remove from pan. Place on cooling rack or across bread pans. Brush top with melted butter. Cool before cutting.

SUCCESS TIPS: 1. For a well shaped loaf, batter must be spread evenly in pan. 2. Too much rising will cause bread to fall. 3. For slicing fresh bread a saw-tooth knife is especially good. Use sawing motion, don't press down. Make slices thicker than usual.

*

POTATO BREAD

1/2 c. cornmeal
1 1/2 c. water
1 c. buttermilk
2 T butter
1 T salt

2 pkgs. dry yeast
1/2 c. warm water
2 T honey
2 c. mashed potatoes
10-11 c. flour

Combine the 1/2 cup cornmeal and the 1 1/2 cups water in saucepan. Bring to boiling; cook and stir till thickened. Remove from heat; stir in buttermilk, the 2 tablespoons butter and salt. Cool. Dissolve yeast in the 1/2 cup warm water, stir in honey. When cornmeal has cooled to lukewarm, add with mashed potatoes to yeast mixture in a large bowl.

Beat in 6 cups of the all purpose flour. Turn out onto lightly floured surface, knead in enough remaining flour to make a stiff dough. Continue kneading till dough is smooth and elastic, 8 to 10 minutes.

Place dough in large greased bowl, turning once to grease surface. Cover and let rise in a warm place till double (about 1 1/2 hours). Punch down dough; divide into 4 or 5 portions. Shape each portion into a flat round loaf. Place on baking sheets. With a sharp knife make three diagonal slashes across each loaf, about 1/4 inch deep. Cover, let rise till nearly double (about 45 minutes). Bake at 350 degrees for 45 minutes or till done.

*

TOMATO BREAD

1/4 c. lukewarm water	3 T dry onion flakes
1 1/2 pkgs. yeast	1 t dry garlic flakes
2 c. tomato juice	1 t celery seed
2 T butter	6 1/2 to 7 cups
3 t sugar	flour
2 1/2 t salt	

Dissolve yeast in lukewarm water with 1 teaspoon sugar. Stir well.

In saucepan heat tomato juice, butter, rest of sugar and salt. Cool. Add to yeast mixture. Add onion, garlic and celery seed. Beat. Add flour one cup at a time, mixing well after each addition.

Knead on floured board for several minutes (8 to 10) until satiny and elastic. Place in greased bowl, turn to grease top, cover and let stand for about 1 hour until double in bulk. Punch down and knead a few minutes.

Shape into three loaves and place in greased loaf pans. Let rise again until double in bulk, about 45 minutes.

Bake in preheated 350 degree oven for 45 to 50 minutes. Don't let bread get too dark. Grease tops when removed from oven. Cool on racks.

*

Michigan was the first state to establish roadside picnic tables.

Fayette Iron Words, Fayette

desserts

DUTCH APPLE PIE

Pastry for 10" pie	1 c. brown sugar
6 apples	1 c. flour
3 T sugar	1/2 c. butter
1 1/2 t cinnamon	1/4 c. cream

Line a 10" pie pan with your favorite pastry. Slice into it the peeled and cored apples. Combine the sugar and cinnamon and mix with apples. Now mix together the brown sugar and flour and cut the butter into this, working it till it is the consistency of coarse crumbs. Spread this over the top of the apples, and then pour the cream slowly over all. Bake at 400 degrees for 15 minutes, then reduce heat to 350 degrees for 30 minutes. Serve with whipped cream or ice cream if desired.

*

BLUEBERRY CRISP

4 c. blueberries	1/3 c. brown sugar
1/3 c. sugar	1/3 c. flour
2 t lemon juice	3/4 c. quick cooking
4 T butter	oats

Put blueberries in deep, greased baking dish and sprinkle with sugar and lemon juice. Cream butter and brown sugar, add flour and oats and spread mixture over the blueberries. Bake at 375 degrees for 35 to 40 minutes. Serve hot or cold with plain or whipped cream.

*

BLUEBERRY GINGERBREAD

3/4 c. blueberries	1/2 c. sour cream
1/3 c. butter	2 c. flour
1/2 c. brown sugar	1 t baking soda
1 egg	1 1/2 t ginger
1 c. molasses	1/2 t salt

Preheat oven to 350 degrees. Butter a 9" square baking pan. Toss berries in small amount of flour and set aside.

Cream butter and sugar. Add egg and beat until light colored. Add molasses and sour cream to butter mixture. Sift flour, soda, ginger, and salt together and add alternately with molasses-sour cream mixture.

Mix only enough to blend ingredients. Add blueberries, folding them in lightly. Spoon batter into pan. Bake for 40 minutes or until cake pulls away from sides of pan. Serve warm.

*

MELON PIE

9" baked pastry shell	1/2 c. heavy cream, whipped
1 3-oz. pkg. lemon gelatin	1 c. cubed cantaloupe well drained
1 c. cubed watermelon well drained	1 c. cubed honeydew melon well drained

Prepare gelatin according to package directions, using only 1 1/2 cups of water. Chill until slightly thickened. Fold in whipped cream and melons. Turn into baked pastry shell. Chill several hours or until firm.

*

CARROT BROWNIES

1/2 c. butter
1 1/2 c. light brown sugar
2 eggs
2 c. flour

2 t baking powder
1/2 t salt
1/4 t cinnamon
2 c. grated carrots
1/2 c. chopped walnuts

Preheat oven to 350 degrees.
In a saucepan melt butter. Add sugar and stir until well blended. Remove from heat and beat in eggs. Beat in remaining ingredients except nuts. Pour mixture into two 8"x8" greased pans. Sprinkle chopped walnuts over mixture in each pan. Bake for 30 minutes. Cut each pan into 9 squares.

*

CARROT CUSTARD

1 lb. carrots, pared
    and cut into 1" pieces
1 c. milk
3 eggs, beaten
1/2 c. light brown sugar

1 t cinnamon
1 t nutmeg
1/2 t ground cloves
1/8 t salt

Preheat oven to 350 degrees.
Place carrots in 1 cup boiling water, cover tightly and cook 10 minutes or until tender. Drain. Puree carrots in blender with milk. Pour into a medium bowl. Add remaining ingredients and beat until blended. Pour into six 2/3-cup buttered custard cups. Place in oven in a shallow baking dish. Add boiling water 1" deep and bake for 35-40 minutes. Serve warm or chilled. Garnish with whipped cream if desired. Serves 6.

*

APPLE CHERRY PIE

2 crust 9" pastry
1 1/3 c. sugar
1/4 c. flour
1 c. tart red cherries

2 c. sliced apples
1/4 t cinnamon
3 T butter

Mix together sugar, flour, cherries, apples, and cinnamon. Place into pastry lined pie pan. Dot with butter. Add top crust. Bake at 400 degrees for 40-50 minutes.

*

BLACK CHERRY YOGURT PIE

2 8-oz. containers
   black cherry yogurt
½ pt. whipped cream,
   whipped & sweetened

1/2 - 3/4 c. cut-up black
   cherries
9" graham cracker crust

Fold together yogurt, whipped cream and cherries. Spoon into prepared crust. Freeze 4 or 5 hours. Place in refrigerator about 30 minutes before serving. Serve with additional whipped cream, if desired.

*

Michigan has a greater variety of minerals-- metallic and non-metallic--than any area of comparable size in the world.

COTTAGE CHEESE CUPCAKES

1/2 c. butter	2 c. flour
2 c. brown sugar	1 t salt
1 t grated lemon peel	1/2 t baking soda
1 egg	1 c. raisins
2 c. cottage cheese	1/2 c. chopped nuts

Cream butter and 1 cup brown sugar together until light and fluffy. Add lemon peel and egg, beating well. Add cottage cheese and remaining cup brown sugar; mix well. Sift together flour, salt and baking soda; add to cottage cheese mixture 1/3 at a time, beating well after each addition. Fold in raisins and nuts. Fill paper baking cups in muffin tin 2/3 full. Bake at 350 degrees for about 20 minutes or until done.

*

BREAD PUDDING

8 slices day-old bread	1 t ground cinnamon
3/4 c. raisins	1/4 t ground nutmeg
3 eggs, beaten	1/8 t salt
3/4 c. sugar	4 c. milk
2 t vanilla	

Tear bread into ½" pieces and place in ungreased 3-quart casserole. Mix eggs, sugar, vanilla, cinnamon, nutmeg and salt in mixing bowl; add milk and beat well. Mix raisins and bread pieces in casserole. Pour milk over bread and raisins. Bake at 325 degrees until table knife inserted halfway between center and edge comes out clean, about 1 hour. Serves 10.

*

HONEY CANDY

1 c. sugar   1 c. honey

Boil ingredients slowly until candy thermometer reaches 265 degrees. Pour onto buttered plate. When cool, stretch candy until light tan and hard. Cut into small pieces.

*

MAPLE CREAMS

1 1/2 c. maple syrup   Pinch salt
1/2 c. heavy cream   Walnut halves

In a heavy saucepan combine syrup, cream, and salt. Bring to a boil, stirring until well blended, then cook until a soft ball stage (236 degrees). Do not stir while it is boiling. Pour syrup into another pan and let stand until lukewarm (110 degrees). Then heat syrup until it becomes light in color and begins to set. Roll a teasponful at a time in palms of the hands and place on buttered baking sheet. Press a walnut into each round, flattening it slightly. Makes 2/3 pound.

*

MAPLE SNOW

Heat syrup to 230 degrees. Pour onto clean, fresh snow (or shaved ice).

*

CREAM CHEESE MINTS

1 lb. powdered sugar
1 3-oz. pkg. cream
   cheese

1/2 t mint extract
Food coloring (if
   desired)

    Mix all ingredients. Roll into small balls
and either press into molds or eat as it.

*

DEEP-DISH PEAR PIE

2 1/2 lb. pears
3/4 c. light brown sugar
3 T flour
1/4 t salt
Dash ground cloves
1/8 t nutmeg

1/3 c. heavy cream
2 T lemon juice
2 T butter
Pastry for 1-crust pie
Heavy cream or vanilla
   ice cream

    Halve pears lengthwise; remove core and stems.
Pare and slice to make 6 cups. In small bowl,
combine brown sugar, flour, salt, cloves and
nutmeg. Stir in 1/3 c. cream. Place sliced
pears in a 9" deep pie plate. Sprinkle with
lemon juice, add cream mixture and stir. Dot
with butter. Preheat oven to 400 degrees.
Place pastry over fruit in baking dish. Press
pastry to edge of dish. Bake for 35-40 minutes.

*

❖❖❖

*The Nation's first regularly scheduled airline
began operation between Grand Rapids and Detroit in
1926.*

PEACHES AND CREAM

4 peaches, peeled
1 c. sherry
1 T sugar

1 T red-currant jelly
1 pt. vanilla ice cream

Cut peaches in half and remove pits. Heat sherry and sugar with pits and peach halves. Simmer for 30 minutes. Remove pits. Put peaches in flat dish and chill. Add jelly to wine mixture and cook until syrupy. Chill. Fill peach halves with ice cream and pour wine sauce over. Serves 4.

*

PLUM CUSTARD PIE

1/2 c. butter
3/4 c. brown sugar
1 c. flour
1/2 t salt
1/4 t baking powder
1/2 t ground cinnamon

1 can (1 pound, 1 ounce) purple plums, drained, halved, pitted
1 egg, slightly beaten
1 c. light cream

Beat butter and sugar in a small bowl until smooth. Sift flour, salt, baking powder, and cinnamon. Blend into sugar mixture. Press evenly on bottom and about 1 inch up sides of 9" pie dish. Arrange plum halves on shell. Combine egg and cream, pour over plums. Bake at 375 degrees for 30-40 minutes or until custard is set. Serves 4.

*

PUMPKIN PARFAIT SQUARES

1 1/2 c. graham cracker
   crumbs
1/4 c. melted butter
1/4 c. sugar
1 1/2 c. pumpkin
1/2 c. brown sugar

1/2 t salt
1 t cinnamon
1/4 t ginger
1/8 t cloves
1 qt. vanilla ice cream
   softened

Mix graham cracker crumbs, melted butter and sugar. Press into bottom of 9" square pan. Combine pumpkin with brown sugar, salt, cinnamon, ginger and cloves and mix well.

Blend into softened ice cream. Pour into crumb-lined pan, cover with foil and freeze several hours or until firm. About 15 minutes before serving time, remove from freezer to soften slightly.

*

RASPBERRY COBBLER

4 c. raspberries
2/3 c. sugar
1/2 t lemon juice
2 T butter
11/2 c. biscuit mix

3 T melted butter
1 egg, slightly beaten
1/2 c. milk
Whipped cream or ice
   cream

Preheat oven to 400 degrees. Grease a 10x6½" baking dish. Toss berries lightly with sugar and lemon juice. Place in baking dish. Dot with 2 tablespoons butter. Combine biscuit mix, melted butter, egg and milk. With a spoon, drop dough over fruit. Bake 30 to 35 minutes. Serve warm with whipped cream or ice cream. Serves 6.

*

RHUBARB CREAM PIE

9" pie shell with
   lattice top
1 1/2 c. sugar
1/4 c. flour
3/4 t nutmeg
Pinch salt

3 eggs
4 c. rhubarb
2 T butter

Mix sugar, flour, nutmeg, and salt. Beat with eggs. Cut rhubarb into 1" pieces. Pour filling into shell. Top with lattice crust. Bake at 400 degrees, 50-60 minutes.

*

RHUBARB CREAM CAKE

1 c. cream
1 egg
3/4 c. sugar
1 1/4 c. flour
1/8 t nutmeg

1 1/2 t baking powder
2 c. rhubarb, cut into
   2" pieces
1/4 c. sugar
1 t cinnamon

Beat cream, egg and sugar. Add flour, baking powder, and nutmeg. Pour in greased 8" square cake pan. Spread rhubarb over cake. Bake 40 minutes in 375 degree oven. Sprinkle sugar and cinnamon on top. Return to oven for 5 more minutes. Serve with cream.

*

SOYBEAN PIE

9" unbaked pie shell
2 c. cooked soybeans
1 c. sugar
1/4 t salt
1 1/2 t cinnamon
1/2 t ginger

3/4 t nutmeg
1/2 t allspice
1/2 t vanilla
3 eggs
1 c. evaporated milk
1/2 c. pecans

Place all ingredients except pecans into blender. Blend until smooth. Add pecans. Pour into pie shell. Bake at 450 degrees for 10 minutes then 30 minutes at 350 degrees or until a knife inserted in the center comes out clean.

*

GLAZED STRAWBERRY PIE

Baked 9" pie shell
1 qt. strawberries
1 3 oz.-pkg. cream
   cheese, softened

1 1/2 c. strawberry
   juice
1 c. sugar
3 T cornstarch

Spread cream cheese over bottom of pastry shell. Cover with half of the berries. Mash and strain rest of berries until juice is extracted. Bring juice to boil. Stir in sugar and cornstarch. Cook over low heat, stirring constantly, until boiling. Boil 1 minute. Pour over berries in pie shell. Chill 2 hours. Just before serving, decorate with whipped cream.

*

STRAWBERRY CAKE

1 c. flour, sifted
1/2 c. sugar
2 t baking powder
Dash of salt
1 egg

2 T melted butter
1/2 c. milk
1 1/2 c. firm strawberries

Sift flour, sugar, baking powder and salt together. Add egg, butter and milk and beat for two minutes. Pour into a greased 8" square pan. Top with sliced strawberries. Sprinkle with topping of 1/2 c. flour, 1/2 c. sugar, 1/4 c. butter, and 1/4 c. chopped nuts. Bake in a 375 degree oven for 35 minutes.

*

STRAWBERRY-TOMATO PIE

10" unbaked pie shell
   with lattice top
1 qt. strawberries
1 c. sugar
4 tomatoes, peeled and
   cubed

6 T flour
1/4 t cinnamon
3 T sugar
3 T butter

Mix strawberries and sugar. Let stand until juice is drawn out, about 1 hour. Pour half the strawberries and juice into pie shell. Sprinkle with half the flour and cinnamon. Top with half of tomatoes and half the sugar. Dot with half the butter. Repeat the layers. Cover with lattice top. Bake at 450 degrees for 15 minutes. Lower heat to 400 degrees and bake 25 minutes. Chill and serve with whipped cream.

*

A CHRISTMAS ON MACKINAC ISLAND IN 1800

by Elizabeth Therese Baird

The Catholic faith prevailing, it followed as a matter of course that the special holidays of the church were always observed in a memorable, pleasant manner in one's own family, in which some friends and neighbors would participate. Some weeks before Christmas, the denizens of the island met in turn at each other's home, and read the prayers, chanted psalms, and unfailingly repeated the litany of the saints. On Christmas Eve, both sexes would read and sing, the service lasting till midnight. After this, a reveillon (midnight treat) would be partaken of by all. The last meeting of this sort which I attended, was at our own home, in 1823. This affair was considered the high feast of the season, and no pains were spared to make the accompanying meal as good as the island afforded. The cooking was done at an open fire. I wish I could remember in full the bill of fare; however, I will give all that I recall. We will begin with the roast pig; roast goose; chicken pie; round of beef, a la mode; pattes d'ours (bear's paws, called so from the shape, and made of chopped meat in crust, corresponding to rissoles); sausage; head-cheese; small-fruit perserves; small cakes.

A CHRISTMAS is a passage from REMINISCENSES OF EARLY DAYS IN MACKINAC ISLAND, a diary written by Mrs. Baird about her childhood days in the early 1800s. Mrs. Baird was the daughter of a Scottish fur trader and granddaughter of an Ottawa chief. She was also of French ancestry, as can be seen by this passage.

Such was the array. No one was expected to partake of every dish, unless he chose. Christmas was observed as a holy-day. The children were kept at home, and from play, until nearly night-time, when they would be allowed to run out and bid their friends a "Merry Christmas", spending the evening, however, at home with the family, the service of prayer and song being observed as before mentioned. All would sing; there was no particular master-- it was the sentiment that was so pleasing to us; the music we did not care so much for.

As soon as *la fete de Noel*, or Christmas-tide, had passed, all the young people were set at work to prepare for New Year's. Christmas was not the day to give and receive presents; this was reserved for New Year's. On the eve of that day, great preparations were made by a certain class of elderly men, usually fishermen, who went from house to house in grotesque dress, singing and dancing. Following this they would receive gifts. This ended the last day of the year. After evening prayer in the family, the children would retire early.

At the dawn of the New Year, each child would go to the bedside of its parents to receive their benediction -- a most beautiful custom. My sympathies always went out to children who had no parents near.

* * *

Mackinac Island means horses and fudge to most people today, although Elizabeth Therese Baird just let us know there's been a lot more to the unique island.

In MICHIGAN COOKING...AND OTHER THINGS I came up with some Mackinac Island-style fudge. Since then I've collected some more fudge recipes. While these probably won't taste like the half-pound of fudge you devoured last summer on the Island, these are pretty good.

Most of all, have fun making them.

* * *

WALNUT CARMEL FUDGE

2 c. walnuts
2 c. sugar

4 c. sugar
2 c. milk
2 t vanilla

Chop walnuts and set aside. Pour 2 c. sugar in a large, heavy skillet and cook over low heat. Keep the sugar moving with the back of a wooden spoon until it melts. Remove from heat and set aside.

Stir 4 c. sugar and milk over low heat in a saucepan until sugar is dissolved. Heat to boiling and add the melted sugar very slowly, stirring constantly. Put in a candy thermometer and cook, stirring occasionally until mixture reaches 234 degrees. Remove from heat and cool, being careful not to stir or jar the pan. When cool enough to touch, add 2 t vanilla. Beat until mixture loses gloss. Quickly, stir in chopped nuts and pour into a buttered pan. When cool, cut into pieces.

*

NO-COOK FUDGE

4 1-oz. unsweetened   Pinch salt
  chocolate squares   3 T milk
2 T melted butter   1 T vanilla
1 lb. powdered sugar

   Melt chocolate and butter over low heat.
In bowl stir sugar, salt, and milk until smooth.
Stir in melted chocolate and vanilla. Spread
on buttered plate and cut into squares.

*

MILLION-DOLLAR FUDGE

(of Mamie Eisenhower fame)

1 13½-oz. can evaporated   1 12-oz. bar sweet
  milk   chocolate
4 1/2 c. sugar   1 8-oz. jar marsh-
2 T butter   mallow cream
Dash salt   2 1/2 c. chopped
1 12-oz. pkg. chocolate   walnuts
  chips

   Bring milk, sugar, butter and salt to a
boil. Stir and boil 7 minutes. Mix remaining
ingredients in large bowl. Pour milk mixture
in. Beat fudge until creamy. Spread in
buttered 9" square pan. Cool. Cut in squares.

*

INDEX
(listed by agricultural products)

ABOUT THE AUTHOR

CAROLE EBERLY, a former newspaper reporter for the
Charlevoix Courier and *United Press International*
at the capitol in Lansing, is editor/publisher of
Eberly's MICHIGAN JOURNAL and owner of *Eberly Press*.
She lives with her husband, John, and daughter,
Jessica, and three cats in East Lansing where everyone gets into the act when a new cookbook is
written--from tasting to reading copy (she has
very unusual cats).

Other *EBERLY PRESS* Publications:

MICHIGAN COOKING...AND OTHER THINGS. A unique
collection of recipes based on Michigan's agri-
culture, witty articles by Michigan writers and
illustrations of Michigan points of interest.
Plastic spiral binding, 112 pages. $4.95.

101 APPLE RECIPES. Apple pizza, apple quiche,
paper bag apple pie, you name it--it's here.
48 pages. $1.95.

COLONIAL FIREPLACE COOKING & EARLY AMERICAN RECIPES.
The cooking teacher at Henry Ford's Greenfield
Village shares her secrets of colonial cooking
and tells you how to recreate her famous authentic
dishes using your own kitchen. Plastic spiral
binding, 96 pages. $4.95.

Other *EBERLY PRESS* Books:

Brownie Recipes Cream cheese brownies supreme, chocolate chip coconut bars, Jessica's mocha-mint caramel downfall, double frosted bourbon brownies... and more than 170 others. Throw out your bathroom scale, move your waistband over an inch. $5.95

Our Michigan: Ethnic Tales & Recipes Canadian butter tarts, Czech kolache, Hungarian linzer slices, Irish coffee, Polish pierogie, Italian ricotta cheesecake, and 150 more ethnic dishes. Fascinating tales about the people who settled Michigan from all over the world. Historical photos. $6.95

Early American Recipes Irish coffee pudding, Shaker lemon pie, hot mustard bread, switchel, Southern spiced tea, dozens more mouth-watering recipes by a Greenfield Village cooking instructor. Beautiful pen and ink illustrations. $4.95

101 Apple Recipes Apple pizza, apple quiche, paper bag apple pie, you name it - it's here. $2.50

101 Fruit Recipes German apple pancake, apricot coconut chews, peach pecan pie, rhubarb cream cake, blueberry coffeecake...101 recipes in all. $2.50

101 Vegetable Recipes The book you can count on when it's your turn to bring the vegetable dish to the school picnic. The cookbook that makes kids like vegetables inspite of themselves. $2.50

101 Cherry Recipes Black cherry cream pie, cherry jelly pie, black cherry biscuits, cherry bounce. $2.50

Please add $1 for postage and handling.

EBERLY PRESS
430 N. Harrison
East Lansing, MI 48823